relationship resonance

positively connect personally, professionally and spiritually

Doug Hacking

WESTBOW
P R E S S®
A DIVISION OF THOMAS NELSON
& ZONDERVAN

WestBow Press books may be ordered through booksellers or by contacting:

WestBow Press
A Division of Thomas Nelson & Zondervan
1663 Liberty Drive
Bloomington, IN 47403
www.westbowpress.com
1 (866) 928-1240

ISBN: 978-1-4908-9362-4 (sc)
ISBN: 978-1-4908-9363-1 (hc)
ISBN: 978-1-4908-9361-7 (e)

Library of Congress Control Number: 2015911168

Print information available on the last page.

WestBow Press rev. date: 08/26/2015

contents

dedication

First and foremost to God. Thank you for the love, guidance, encouragement and blessing me with all the resources to create this book.

To my beloved wife, Mary Ann. Thank you for believing in me, supporting me, pushing me, and guiding me. You have given me life's riches. "A wife of noble character who can find? She is worth far more than rubies" (Proverbs 31:10).

To my children. Thank you for teaching me something every day and giving my heart a whole new meaning of love.

To my mother, who tirelessly worked several jobs simultaneously to make ends meet. Thank you for teaching me the value of hard work.

To my father, who would valiantly defend me and help me make award-winning school projects. Thank you for teaching me several of life's lessons.

To my uncles, Mike and Perry. Thank you for being great positive role models and raising the bar.

To my stepfather, Charlie. Thank you for all the trust and support.

To my pastor, Craig Groeschel. Thank you for helping me become a fully devoted follower of Christ.

And special thanks to my wife, Mary Ann, for all the time proof-reading, picture formatting, and head shot! To my daughter, Meredith, for creating the chapter illustrations; you are only ten and already such an amazing artist! To Cherry Tree Visual for the cover design, chapter headings, and charts. And to everyone at WestBow Press for all the assistance in putting it all together. I couldn't have asked for a better team.

introduction

Just like climbing Kilimanjaro, relationships are expeditions with easy and hard stretches; hikers who make those climbs will do so much more smoothly if they are well prepared. They don't want to start their journeys without water bottles, proper clothing, sleeping bags, and backpacks. Being unequipped and trying to figure it out as they go would almost certainly result in a big letdown.

Though all this seems obvious, this neglectful, learn-as-we-go approach is so common in our relationships. How many relational classes were we exposed to in grade school or as adults? I can't remember any. We're just expected to be good at probably the most important aspect of life—building strong relationships as we interact with people.

The purpose of this book is to EQUIP you with the tools to make a positive impact as you connect with others. I have shared a system that helps your relationships resonate actions that feel personally meaningful and important, thus strengthening your personal, professional, and spiritual bonds.

The need for this is greater these days than perhaps ever before. Technology has us communicating via text messages and e-mails while we multitask at a frantic pace. Face to face interactions are on the decline. Divorce rates are ridiculously high, and everyone is turning to computers to match him or her up with someone. What if we get a chance with a perfect match but mess it up because we were ill equipped to handle the relationship? Are we prepared to stay that course?

Throughout my entire childhood, my parents had the same washer and dryer, microwave, lawn mower, and Christmas lights. If something was broken, my dad fixed it. If clothes ripped, my mom mended them. But today, when things break after a year or two, the mentality is to simply replace them with newer models. Hey! Isn't it time for an upgrade? The problem is that this thought process can easily spill over into our relationships. Then when we make mistakes and damage a relationship, instead of investing in the effort to mend it, we often simply consider replacing it with another relationship. But the good news about the mistakes we make is that they show us what we need to learn.[1]

When I have looked back at my struggles, I have usually always found areas in which I could have been relationally better. However, during the time of my trials, I routinely and conveniently played the victim. It was easy and quite common to find fault with the other people involved; I blamed them for the problems or used them as excuses for my poor judgment. But implicating others did little for the situations or gave me hope for the future. And when others heard or saw me refusing to take responsibility for myself, it usually had a negative effect on my relationships with them as well.

One of the biggest reasons we fail to take responsibility for our poor relationships is because we all tend to deceive ourselves. It's much easier to tell ourselves *It can't be my fault* as we point our fingers at the others involved. Or we tell ourselves, *I was doing all these things for them* when our motives were much more selfish. And we often don't realize we're just fooling ourselves.

Aware of this, King David constantly invited God to search his heart and the hidden motives within as he led the nation of Israel. The only thing worse than being ignorant is being ignorant of our own ignorance, when we don't even know what we don't know. What we do know is that "the heart is deceitful" and can fool even its owner. Much damage can be inflicted from that place.[2]

The above passage comes from *Interrupted* by Jen Hatmaker. She made reference to the Bible and the book *Leadership and Self-Deception* by the Arbinger Institute. An employee gave me a copy of the *Self-Deception* book early on in my managerial career in an attempt to teach me how I was fooling myself in my working relationships. I was so deceived that I refused to read it and left it on our nightstand to collect dust. Thankfully, my wife became so fascinated with it that she read it in a couple of days and encouraged me to read it as well. That book opened our eyes and made us much more accountable for our actions.

When you hold yourself accountable for your thoughts and deeds, good things happen. People are drawn to others who own the responsibility for their problems. When I look at the damaged or broken relationships in my life, I ask myself, *How could I have prevented this?* and *What can I do better in the future?* as I recall the methods I have confidence in based on past success.

What I have learned from many other books, workshops, conferences, and good old trial and error has allowed me to manage very well in several relational arenas. I have received many awards and recognitions that I credit to the positive connections I made along the way. The most recent award was for being an outstanding preceptor that I received from the University of Oklahoma College of Pharmacy, an award given to faculty based on students' feedback after working with me as they prepare for graduation. I was also awarded the Pharmacy Manager Paragon award by CVS pharmacy, which is given to pharmacists who consistently and passionately represent the qualities and performance of the company. I attribute these awards not to my pharmaceutical and business knowledge but rather to my emphasis on the relationships with my patients, students, and coworkers.

I've spent the last twenty years analyzing my failures and successes while applying knowledge from research and mentors to improve my relationships. As a result, I've created a working system that captures the essence of all my findings. I call it Relationship Resonance, and it is composed of the EQUIP model and Personality Matrix. The EQUIP model contains five components: Encouragement, Quality Time, Understanding, Investing, and Physical Touch.

After learning about these tools and how to use them, you make the daily effort to EQUIP your relationships. You can use anywhere from one to all five components in any interaction. For example, you may realize a business relationship is lacking understanding and thus use an active listening approach (explained in the "Understanding" chapter) in your next interaction. The result is the potential for a positive, resonating impact on the relation.

I picked the EQUIP components after trying to recall what has made my best relationships flourish. I remember many of the smiles and positive comments they have blessed me with. These elements just seemed to resonate with everyone and brought out the best in us all. They have surrounded me with positive and productive people.

The second part of the Relationship Resonance system involves utilizing the EQUIP elements as you move through the Personality Matrix. Each matrix consists of a four-quadrant model founded on the currently popular personality temperaments that Galen (AD 150) theorized about over 2,000 years ago. I then tie the four quadrants together with a common theme to make the personality concepts easier to understand and apply.

For example, I have a coach, quarterback, referee, and cheerleader matrix. After realizing you may have been a "coach" in a relationship, you may make the effort to move through the matrix and apply some referee, quarterback, and/or cheerleader qualities. (This is further explained in the "Personality Matrix" chapter.)

As I've worked on the system over time, three things became clear. First, the keys to great relationships all stem from the Bible. There is nothing new under the sun when it comes to our dealings with others. The Good Book contains accounts from over 2,000 years ago of everything we're going through today. If you tell me any type of positive action that has helped you in a relationship, I bet I can find a Bible verse to support it. Interestingly, this revelation became apparent to me only recently when I finally started attending church regularly.

I grew up the son of an atheist father and a nonpracticing Christian mother. I had no idea about even the most basic information in the Bible. I have always believed in God and was drawn to learn more about Christ, but I gave that a very low priority in my YOLO (**Y**ou **O**nly **L**ive **O**nce) life. It wasn't until I was over thirty and started attending Life Church regularly that

I completely reversed my priorities and put God first. When I did that, everything else just fell into place, including my relationships.

As I would sit and listen to my pastor, Craig Groeschel, preach, I would always identify parts of his message that would fit and enhance my EQUIP model's relevance. That's when I learned all my previous work on this book and leadership research was already in the Bible. To seal the deal for me, Craig would often randomly use the word *equip* in his messages. Every time Craig used it, my wife nudged me to encourage more writing. The more I attended, the better this book became. It went from a few hundred words to thousands. It was as if God had turned my loaf and two fish into a feast.

My second epiphany about relationships was that they work like bank accounts. We need to continually make deposits to cover our withdrawals. By withdrawals, I mean all the bad things we do that intentionally or unintentionally hurt our relationships. I feel I could be a relational expert after all my time and effort in this arena, yet I still frequently do things to hurt people. I get impatient, frustrated, jealous, and angry just as everyone else does at times. I say things that are misunderstood and create problems when I was just trying to joke around or encourage others.

So, to keep the relationships in a positive account balance, I frequently deposit positive relational builders in the form of my EQUIP components. For example, after I lose patience and became frustrated with one of my children and say something I regret, I make it a priority to get in some physical touch and quality time with that child for the remainder of the day. I put in more than I took out. Just as a guitar has to be strummed to give off beautiful music, we need to continually strum our relationships to keep them in resonating harmony.

Keeping a surplus of positive deposits in others' accounts also softens the blow when I inevitably make a withdrawal because the relationship is already strong. That brings me to my last observation: it takes a lot of work to improve and strengthen relationships. When I'll have serious talks with my children later in life, I want to be sure I've built a strong relationship well beforehand; you can't just pick up a book like this and fix a broken relationship overnight. If you've been making years of withdrawals, it could take years of deposits to get a relationship positive again. But there's no better time to start EQUIPing than now.

I'm not writing *the* book on relationships; that's what the Bible is. I'm just trying to give others a method they can immediately apply to any relational situation. Whether you're a Christian or a follower of another religion, my hopes are that the Relationship Resonance system can help you. You can skip the verses and personal stories in this book and just focus on the nuts and bolts of the contents.

I wish you well in your journey and pray this book will help to strengthen all your relationships—personal, professional, and spiritual.

chapter 1
encouragement

Most of us, swimming against the tides of trouble
the world knows nothing about, need only a bit of
encouragement—and we will make the goal.
—Robert Collier

In 1983, Jim Valvano led a group of ordinary basketball players to a nine-game winning streak that ended in perhaps the greatest basketball victory of the twentieth century. If Valvano's team had lost any of those nine games, its season would have abruptly ended.

During that famous run, Valvano's team was dubbed the Cardiac Pack because in most of those matches, they were losing with under a minute to play. In the final game, for the championship, the team made the winning shot with one second remaining.

Valvano's team made the clutch shots where the competition failed. His players believed in themselves through every adverse situation; they never gave up even when winning appeared to be out of reach.

Midway through the streak, the opposing team was already celebrating its victory on the sidelines with little time remaining. The celebration suddenly turned into shocked disbelief when the Cardiac Pack won. Fifty million viewers of the championship game shared that shock when David slew Goliath in an outcome no expert could have predicted. Valvano's team beat a group of five ultra-athletic superstars dubbed the Five-Slamma-Jamma led by a literal giant and the MVP of the tournament.

The only people who knew they would win that day were the members of the Cardiac Pack and their coach. They had practiced the traditional victory ceremony of cutting down the nets several times prior to the championship game.

From day one, Valvano pumped his players full of encouragement in the form of positive affirmation, enthusiasm, smiles, and hugs, some would even say in an excessive manner. The other coaches in the league thought Valvano was overly enthusiastic, and they criticized him for it.

But Valvano believed in his players and let them wholeheartedly know that at every opportunity. His players in turn believed in themselves and achieved legendary greatness. That's the power of encouragement! And with a little help, you'll soon be cutting down some nets of your own.[3]

The Cardiac Pack's success exemplifies proverbs 18:21, "The tongue has the power of life and death, and those who love it will eat its fruit." Valvano's words inspired his players to overcome immense adversity and achieve greatness. The assistant coach has said that Valvano's pregame pep talks took his players' abilities to new levels. He spoke life-giving words to his team when everyone else was saying his players were dead in the water.

Valvano never considered or planted the seed of a scenario in which his players missed shots. When the games were hanging on the outcome of a free throw by one of Valvano's players, he always gave instructions for what to do after the shot was made. He would make statements such as, "Okay, after we make this one, here's what we do next."

I ask you, what are your words doing? Is your tongue building people up or tearing them down? Are you planting the seeds of success or failure? Are you pouring courage into those around you, encouraging them, giving them the power to think, speak, try, and do things without fear? Are you letting them confidently take the last shot with the game's outcome hanging on the result? Or are you draining courage from people, discouraging them, paralyzing them to not think, speak, try, and do things because you're sure they'll fail you?

Unfortunately, discouragement can resonate for a long time as we replay in our minds what was done or said that hurt us. If the hurt is too great or the discouragement continues, the result can be the death of a relationship. Many times, showing grace and forgiveness for someone's actions is easier said than done.

Fortunately for me, my wife is one of those amazing people who can always find a way to forgive me for my discouragement. She tries to understand where my words and actions stem from and finds the grace to forgive me as we discuss the issues. And through my discussions with her, I've discovered that many times, I just unintentionally sent the wrong message.

Sometimes, we think we're encouraging people, but instead, we're discouraging them by using the wrong words or approaches. I've noticed that many times what people intend to accomplish is the opposite of what they do accomplish. I'll discuss this 180-degree differential of how people believe they're being perceived and how they are perceived further in the "Personality Matrix" chapter. But for now, let me share some examples I've personally experienced on both ends of discouragement: being discouraged and discouraging others.

> My father gave me the greatest gift anyone could give another person, he believed in me.
> —Jim Valvano

I have no doubt my father believed in me just as Valvano's father believed in him. However, my dad's approach to conveying his beliefs usually left me upset and frustrated. This isn't a knock against my father; I know his heart was in the right place.

I sometimes see parents, including myself, using similar methods when raising their children. It seems to be an old style passed down through the generations. But here's the example of how I felt discouraged during my last years of grade school.

During my early school days, I never put much effort into making A's. I was able to pass tests and move on by simply paying attention in class. Then, in tenth grade, my teachers started encouraging me to work harder. They gave me loads of positive feedback and life-affirming words, so I stepped up and went for straight A's. I took good notes, paid attention to deadlines, and finished homework before starting any after-school activities. One of my friends looked stunned when I did my trigonometry homework before playing video games with him.

Then the report card came: five A's and one B. The B was in honors biology. I realized that I could have put more effort into that class and that I'd received what I deserved. I still felt good about my accomplishments—until I showed the report card to my dad. All my dad could focus on was the B. I even tried to spin it that I could have received an easy A in regular biology but that I had gone for a bigger challenge.

I truly believe my dad was trying to encourage me to do better. I know he thought I had a lot of potential and wanted the best for me. But the words he used ripped through me like a sword. I was devastated.

The next semester, I was discouraged and frustrated. My grades dropped one by one and got worse each semester. Then, in my final high school semester, I failed a couple of classes and just barely earned enough credits to graduate.

As a young adult, I vowed I would never discourage others. I convinced myself that I was a positive person because I could always tell others how to make things better. But that was the same as focusing on the B. I was constantly finding flaws and offering suggestions for improvement. I was a discouraging nitpicker, the opposite of the positive person I thought I was.

I was hard on everyone but even harder on myself. Any time someone gave me a compliment, I immediately told myself how I could have done better; I discouraged myself even in the midst of praise. I've learned I need to focus on the A's and then watch the B's naturally improve as a result.

Almost every time I've embraced this leadership style, I've enjoyed a lot of success and personal satisfaction. But even today, I still catch myself unintentionally discouraging others. I usually quickly realize my error and try to correct it, but often, the damage has already been done. And unfortunately, as I know all too well, discouraging words can resonate for a long time.

Recently, I discovered I've been discouraging my wife's photography business by repeatedly suggesting she charge more. I see others charge more for lower-quality pictures and offer fewer pictures for purchase. I see my wife's product as worth much more than she charges and feel she almost gives away her pictures. I'm not the only one who believes her work is spectacular. She's had a picture go viral on social media and eventually end up in the national BabyCenter blog.

The problem is that I routinely fail to reinforce how incredible her pictures are and how good of a photographer I consider her. I believe in her ability and constantly brag about her to other people as I pass out her business cards. But all she hears repeatedly is a disappointing "You should've charged more" or an even worse "Maybe you could brighten it up a bit?" She doesn't hear me promoting her to others or my thoughts of amazement or why I think her pictures are valuable. When I see the discouragement on her face as she looks at her work, it kills me. My unseen actions and thoughts are positive, but my tongue betrays me and tears her down.

Unfortunately, when I watch and listen to the world around me, I see that it's more common for people to tear down than to build up. All too often, people are bombarded with negative comments and discouragement, intentional and unintentional, from themselves and others. Too many people prefer to complain rather than praise.

We all do many great things daily, but we usually hear only about what we did wrong or how we could have done something better. I imagine some people can go days without any positive feedback about themselves or their accomplishments.

This is especially true in the workplace. I usually hear from certain managers above me only when some result is less than desirable and even if many other results exceeded expectations. Such continual discouragement can negatively affect the relationships involved. The results are decreased spirit, communication barriers, animosity, decreased productivity, employee turnover, lost friendships, and even divorce. Negative talk often leads to negative results. Even when comments aren't directed toward me personally, I eventually hear them through the grapevine. How many conversations have started with, "Guess what I heard so-and-so say?"

But fortunately, the reverse is also true. Positive talk usually leads to direct and indirect positive results. I have been praised several times by random customers for my kind words to my employees. I had no idea the customers were even listening to my conversation. However, my positive words indirectly enhanced the relationship with the customer and hopefully directly enhanced my relationship with the employee. This resonating phenomenon makes a case for the wise adage, "Praise in public and correct in private."

I've felt the power of being encouraged in public when I run 5Ks. I do so much better running when a large crowd is enthusiastically cheering me on. I run harder for the crowd than I normally would without them. We all do better when people are cheering and encouraging us along the way. Even when my fire is dying down, all it takes is a single spark in the form of a "You can do it!" to turn those embers into a raging inferno.

Hillsong Church, one of the fastest-growing churches in the country, understands the power that encouragement has to keep us in the race. Hillsong's New York City lead pastor, Carl Lentz, disciples to professional athletes and performing artists. Once, Pastor Lentz brought one of his disciples, NBA superstar Kevin Durant, to be interviewed by Life Church's founder and lead pastor Craig Groeschel to discuss spiritual growth. Craig asked Carl what was the one thing he could do to help new believers grow spiritually. Carl said, "Encourage, to be encouraged. Our whole church is about lifting the heads of many, Encourage."[4]

Therefore encourage one another and build each other up...
—1 Thessalonians 5:11

Encourage on a daily basis. Don't wait until the report card comes to encourage the result. Encourage each step of the journey along the way. Encourage in good times and in bad, victory and defeat, others and yourself. Encourage encourage encourage! And remember that even when things look like there is no hope and the game is over, encourage some more.

Don't give up don't ever give up!
—Jim Valvano

How do we encourage? We can encourage people by praising and complimenting them, showing our appreciation, and using positive language.

Praise and Compliments

The easiest way to start encouraging people is with the first component: praise and compliments. A simple "Good job!" has immediate positive impact. This sounds like basic advice, but it's so rare today. My wife can be fueled for days by a random compliment, perhaps a stranger in a grocery store telling her she's doing a great job with the kids.

Encouraging language can resonate for a long time. One of my employees told me that my partner at the pharmacy, Natasha, said I was doing a good job keeping all our medicines in stock. Even three years later, I can still hear those words resonate as I tediously fill out medication order forms. It makes me feel that my work is appreciated, and as a result, I try harder to keep the medicines in stock.

Build others up with praise and compliments, not cheap flattery. The difference is sincerity. Cheap flattery is insincere while praise and compliments are sincere and from the heart. I once worked with a woman who told me, "Hey, nice belt!" I liked that until I heard her giving everyone the same compliment. It quickly lost its effect; I considered it insincere and started wondering if the woman simply had a belt fetish. Most people can tell if someone is giving a sincere compliment. I guess the woman had noticed how compliments could have a positive impact, but she took it too far. Be sure your compliments come from your heart, not your "Nice belt!" machine gun.

My daughter, Meredith, illustrates an example of the power of a sincere compliment. During a hectic Christmas shopping season, our family went to a superstore for some last-minute items. The checkout lines were long. Being in retail myself, I know many customers like to tell you everything wrong with you, your store, and the world as you ring them up. However, as the checker scanned our items, my ten-year-old daughter told her, "Hey, I like your necklace." The checker suddenly transformed from a robot silently and unemotionally scanning item after item into a smiling and beaming person lively with appreciation for the compliment. I have no doubt that Meredith was being completely sincere since she had put jewelry on her Christmas list, and I believe the checker felt the sincerity of the compliment. As we left the store, the energized checker waved and wished us a Merry Christmas. I could see her new enthusiasm continuing while she checked out people behind us. That simple sincere praising of her necklace totally transformed her mood and had a positive effect on her day and ours.

To enhance the positive effect of a compliment, elaborate on it with some specifics to show a deeper understanding. For example, when my daughter draws a picture for me, I can say, "Nice job!" and then follow that up with how I liked the way she used proportions so accurately, which made the 3D affects look realistic.

Another example is when someone comes in early for work. I can say, "Good to see you! Thanks for being on time." I get more specific with, "I like it when you get here before the customers arrive so we can have a smooth start to the day. It makes the whole day better." Being specific with your compliments can enhance their impact.

But encouragement can become excessive if not presented the right way or at the right time. Everyone has different levels of what he or she is comfortable with on the receiving end of praise and compliments. Try to get a feel for your enthusiasm to avoid going over the top.

Once, during my son's soccer game, I noticed he gave me what looked like a high five from across the field. I thought, *Ahh how cute! My son just made a good play and gave his dad a high five.* It wasn't until the car ride home that I learned that wasn't a high five. He told me I was clapping too much and too loudly. He explained how he had held his hand up in hopes I would stop cheering so loud. It wasn't a high five at all but rather a "Dad! Enough!" I realized I had been going overboard on the encouragement, enthusiasm, directing, and volume. He and I agreed on a slightly quieter celebration from me on the sidelines. I wanted him to see my encouragement but not be embarrassed by it.

Appreciation

Another way we encourage others is by showing our appreciation. If someone does something for you, never forget to thank him or her. A thank you is another seemingly obvious relation builder that is nonetheless often overlooked. When you thank someone, that usually makes that person feel encouraged and likely to repeat the nice act.

How many times have you heard someone vent to you that his or her significant other doesn't appreciate all he or she does? If you don't get your courtesy thank you wave after letting a car into gridlocked traffic, do you get upset? Have you ever told someone you don't feel appreciated? All these problems could be prevented with a simple thank you. Why don't we thank enough? The problem dates back to biblical times.

Luke 17 tells the story of Jesus healing ten people inflicted with leprosy, a chronic bacterial infection that causes damage to the skin, limbs, nerves, and eyes. It can leave its victims deformed and unpleasant to say the least. So imagine having this terrible disease and having Jesus heal you. Would you thank Him? Well, Luke recorded that only one of the ten came back to thank Jesus. Jesus asked the one where the other nine were. Such a big miraculous gift for ten but just one thank-you note!

We all know we should thank people, but then there's the problem of doing that. If we don't recognize an act as worthy of a thank you, we naturally won't give one. We should be thankful for everything. Just waking up in the morning to see a new day and spend time with friends and family is a miracle we should be thankful for. But still, I can fail to thank God each day for this blessing. It definitely takes work and discipline, and it seems that the more people are blessed with, the harder it becomes for them to be thankful.

Adam Yenser sums it up best in his stand-up comedy routine.

> I was at Universal Studios and I saw a tourist, who looked like he was from a third world country, admiring that giant fountain they have out front. And I thought, "How would you even explain a giant fountain to someone visiting from a third world country?" Like, "No, sir, you don't put your mouth in there. See here in America, we have so much clean drinkable water that sometimes we just use the extra to decorate. And then what

> we do is take our spare change, which is all the
> money we have after buying everything we could
> possibly want, and then we just throw it in the
> fountain and make a wish for a better life."[5]

We all can get caught up in wanting more while taking everything or everybody in our lives for granted. I could easily list several things my wife does for me and our family each day before I even get out of bed. Thanking her for just one of these acts daily would go a long way toward making her feel more appreciated and raising her spirits. It encourages her to continue to work hard for us. It also encourages her that she made the right decision when she said yes in our driveway after my overly planned and poorly executed marriage proposal. Admittedly, it's as unnatural for me as it is for most people, but I continue to work on being thankful, then thanking her to show appreciation and encourage her.

I work on thanking my employees and customers. The company I work for also knows the importance of thanking customers. We have a huge, six-foot, illuminated thank-you sign above the exit as well as business metrics geared toward thanking customers. They put many resources into this because they know that if customers feel appreciated by a thank you, that will encourage them to come back. We need to put the same resources into our relationships and become that six-foot, illuminated sign for all the people in our lives.

Simply thanking coworkers each day does volumes for relationships and productivity. Pharmacy schools send their students to pharmacies to give them real-world job experience as part of their curricula. Our pharmacy is one of these sites. Almost all the student interns tell me that ours is the only pharmacy that thanks them for coming and helping us with its work; they say the other pharmacies just expect them to come in. They like that we express our appreciation for their time and effort. As a result, they come back more often, work harder, and even apply for positions with our company.

We can expand on appreciation just as we did with praise and compliments. We can say, "Thank you for …" and "This helped me with …" to create a potentially greater positive impact. For example, we can send thank-you notes saying, "Thank you for the gift" or make even a bigger impact with something like, "Thank you for the toy car. Our child enjoys playing with it and is having all kinds of fun with it today. It's even his favorite color yellow! Good job on the selection!"

Appreciation is a powerful relationship builder. Learning to be thankful, recognizing opportunities, and executing appreciation can quickly encourage those around you and improve your relationships.

Positive Language

The last way to encourage is with positive language. This includes content, tone, and body language. The content is the actual words we say or write. They should stem from key positive words such as *can* and *will* instead of negative words such as *can't* and *won't*. Not only will positive words have a better chance of creating a good relationship, they can also prevent a difficult situation from getting out of hand. This is because some negative words can trigger an irrational emotional response.

I first learned about this concept in a business school leadership class when I read a book about dealing with upset customers.[6] The biggest takeaway I got from that book was how negative words can start fights with upset customers and others. After dealing with more than my fair share of upset customers in my life, this knowledge is by far my greatest tool for improving situations.

Imagine an impatient customer coming in to drop off a prescription and asking how long it will take to fill it. If I use negative words such as, "I can't have this ready for at least thirty minutes because it's busy," the customer might get upset. However, if I use a positive language and say, "Even though it's a peak time for us right now, I can speed this up and can have it ready in thirty minutes," my use of *can* instead of *can't* usually keeps customers from becoming upset or defensive. If the customer says he or she can't wait thirty minutes, I offer solutions with positive words such as, "Okay, if you would like to shop in the store or run a quick errand, we can notify you as soon as it's ready, or we will hold onto it until it's more convenient for you to come back." When it comes to refills, saying "I can fax your doctor" instead of "I can't fill this" often keeps everything okay. Such positive words keep situations from becoming hostile, while negative words can discourage people and cause us to lose customers.

This even holds true for my three-year-old at the department store. When he sees something he wants, he will grab it and jump up and down, asking if he can have it. If he hears negative words in my response such as "No" or "You already have too many toys" or "Forget it," he will fall to the floor in a tantrum and leave me with a difficult situation to handle. But if I keep the responses positive and say, "Okay, we can put it on your birthday list" or "Yes, we'll tell Santa about it," I get an "Okay, Dad!" with a smile. My positive words give him hope. I offer one caveat to this rule: if you think the item may end up on a birthday or Christmas list, get the item now or you might end up paying three times the price on eBay in order to keep your promise.

This positive language concept also explains some tough lessons I learned early as a pharmaceutical sales rep. If I wanted a doctor to prescribe my drug rather than the competition's, I had two strategies: I could discourage the doctor from writing the competition's drug by spouting negative facts about its drug, or I could encourage the use of my drug by mentioning the positive benefits it would have for his or her patients. If I used negative words about the competitor's drugs, I would get shut down quickly. If I bashed the competition, I was essentially saying the doctor had been making bad prescribing decisions. That was usually followed by the sound of a door slamming in my face. But if I encouraged the use of my drug by emphasizing its positive benefits, doctors were much more receptive and likely to prescribe my drug. Doctors want the best for their patients, so positive solutions were well received.

You can avoid using negative language even when you're in the middle of correcting someone. Most business manager lessons about correcting behavior or discussing potential areas of improvement usually say to give some positives before bringing up the negatives. This softens the blow and can help keep the other person from becoming defensive.

I've discovered a way to tweak this method to enhance the results. I use needs instead of negs—negatives. For example, if you have employees who are consistently late to work, telling them they are late too much is a negative. Instead, you can tell them you need them to be on time, and then explain the needs or policies of the company. I've found the result is a better acceptance of the correction that doesn't erode the relationship.

Perhaps that greatest and most powerful positive word we can use is *love*. Letting people know you love them is a huge relationship builder. We're quick to shout out how much we love a certain car or movie but are guarded when it comes to using the word *love* when it applies to people or their actions. That's especially true when it comes to men telling other men they love them. But a well-timed, sincere use of this powerful word can resonate for a lifetime.

Spencer Tillman, one of the University of Oklahoma's all-time great running backs and ESPN sports analyst, tells a great story about the powerful impact of the word *love*. His coach, the legendary Barry Switzer, motivated him before one of their biggest rivalry games against Nebraska. Spencer says that while they were in the tunnel leading out to the field into the sight of 80,000 screaming fans, Barry pulled him aside, looked at him with his famous squinted eyes, and said, "Spencer, I love you." No last-minute instructions or "You can do it" or game implications—just a simple, heartfelt "I love you." At first, Spencer thought, *What? I'm trying to get hyped up for eighty thousand fans and you're telling me you love me?* But as the game progressed, the words resonated in his mind. Spencer realized they were exactly what he had needed to hear. He put on an outstanding running performance to display his appreciation and show his coach that he loved him back.[7]

It's not just what we say but also how we say it. In the movie *Hitch*, the main character said communication is 60 percent body language, 30 percent tone, and 10 percent content. I agree. Most of what is important is not the content coming out of your mouth. When I come home and my dog runs to greet me, wagging his tail, jumping, and licking my face, no words are necessary. I know he's excited to see me, and that makes me feel good.

The fact that body language and tone are such huge parts of communication creates a problem with texting or writing. It's difficult to get a feel for the tone of typed words. We try to use emoticons, caps, and punctuation, but many times, these cues are misinterpreted. Unfortunately, more and more communication is being handled through such "faceless" avenues. Use the phone to call someone and schedule more face time; you'll have a greater chance of projecting encouragement and improving the relationship.

Hitch's 60/30/10 rule also explains why when it comes to positive language that the content, tone, and body language must go together naturally. For example, if you ask someone, "How can I help you?" in a sarcastic tone and uninterested body language such as rolling your eyes, that won't do much for improving the relationship. The 90 percent of tone and body language overrides the 10 percent of content; the other person will quickly realize you don't want to help him or her. When body language and tone don't fit with the message, the "bogus alarm" will go off and you won't come across as sincere. Your tone should be genuine, kind, caring, and enthusiastic, not sarcastic, uninterested, mean, or angry.

When I was starting out as a drug rep, I noticed that doctors would frequently tune out and yawn in the middle of my sales pitch. I was a doctor of pharmacy and had a great grasp of the clinical information I was conveying, but my monotone and dull approach was preventing the information from being received. My 10 percent content was good, but my 30 percent tone and 60 percent body language needed improvement. I watched my extremely upbeat and enthusiastic partner, Amie, captivate and dominate conversations and get her message across. Her tone and body language trumped any content I was attempting to convey. In fact, she didn't need much content at all. So I worked on delivering my message in a more enthusiastic tone, and my sales dramatically increased. I was finally encouraging the use of my product.

When customers come into our pharmacy with a complaint, if I try to resolve their problem in a stern, professional tone, I create more problems. Even if my content is 100 percent accurate and relevant, it can easily be overshadowed by my tone and body language. However, if I speak in a kind, caring voice, I can usually resolve the problem without even offering a solution. Just the fact that the patient feels someone cares about his or her problem is often enough.

Anxiety weighs down the heart, but a kind word cheers it up.
—Proverbs 12:25

We have a pharmacy technician, Sarah, with whom I've had the pleasure of working beside for ten years now. She has always been upbeat and in a good mood with a big, gleaming smile and enthusiastic tone even when someone complains about her specifically. Several customers have told me over the years that just hearing her upbeat voice on the phone makes their bad days good. Many pharmacy customers tell me how much they appreciate Sarah as they drop off their prescriptions for their serious medical conditions. Sarah's encouragement is often better than any medicine I can give them.

> A cheerful heart is good medicine, but a
> crushed spirit dries up the bones.
> —Proverbs 17:22

Since we all can't visit Sarah each day, another way to get a daily dose of positive language with a positive tone coming into your life is through a Christian rock music station such as The House FM. I started listening to this station thinking it was "house" or club music. I had spent much time "clubbing it" in my younger days, and thought I would enjoy hearing some of those old songs again. I listened for several minutes before I realized that all the songs were biblically based. The music was what I enjoyed, so I didn't pay attention to the lyrics. But before I knew it, I started enjoying the lyrics. I felt many times that their words were aimed directly at my life. They encouraged me and lifted my spirits.

One song, "Overcomer," by Mandisa, was so powerful that it became my mantra anytime the enemy tried to bring me down. I've spent a majority of my life fearing that I could never succeed in my dreams of writing this book and helping others because of all my past mistakes. I'd committed every sin in the book and many times felt I had taken myself out of the race. But that song reminded me that I had overcome all that and would continue to overcome. I keep my eye on Christ and keep fighting because I know I can achieve all things through Him! The House FM is so encouraging for me that I have a hard time listening to anything else.

When I listen to the other stations that promote sex, drugs, and sin, that's what I think about as I sing along. I've sang along with "Devil Inside" and "Running with the Devil" several times. They used to be two of my favorites, but I now cringe when they come on. I have personally experienced garbage-in garbage-out with my radio selections and now choose to let the station encourage me so I can encourage others.

> Finally, brothers and sisters, whatever is true, whatever
> is noble, whatever is right, whatever is pure, whatever
> is lovely, whatever is admirable-if anything is excellent
> or praiseworthy-think about such things.
> —Philippians 4:8

If we stay with the 60/30/10 rule, body language is the most important factor when it comes to communicating; our bodies often tell the real story. It's easier to change the content of our message in an attempt to fool someone than it is to keep our pupils from dilating or skin from perspiring. People make a living knowing how to read body language to tell if someone is lying about a crime or holding no aces as they bet all their chips. Body language is a science of its own; I recommend your picking up any basic body language book to gain more insight on this important topic. But here are a few encouraging body language basics.

> Smile, for everyone lacks self-confidence and more
> than any other one thing a smile reassures them.
> —Andre Maurois

The quickest and easiest body language to understand is the smile. Smiling is huge when it comes to encouraging. The most frequent complaint I receive on my customer surveys and sometimes even face to face is that I don't smile enough. When customers bring in prescriptions and I smile, what I'm saying is that I'm glad they chose our pharmacy and that I'm encouraging them to come back in the future. On the contrary, if I scowl when they drop off prescriptions, I'm discouraging future business and hurting our relationship. My body language is saying, "Why are you here and bothering me?"

So why don't I always smile? Retail pharmacy is a fast-paced job that requires an immense amount of concentration and work-flow management. My problem is that when I'm concentrating, I'm not smiling. I have to make an effort to not give our customers the wrong impression. Plus, smiling at work is unnatural for me since I'm more of a constant thinker and analyzer. But since it's it so important in building relationships, I'm really working in this area. I've found customer interactions go infinitely better when I start them with a smile.

When I smile, my team and the customers contagiously follow my lead. Of all emotional signals, smiles are the most contagious; they have an almost irresistible power to make others smile in return.[8] When I begin an interaction with a friendly smile, I'm indicating that I'm looking for a pleasant outcome, and others naturally want to help me achieve that goal. Smiles may be ways we have learned over the years to cement alliances and signal we are relaxed and friendly rather than guarded or hostile.[9]

Besides the obvious frowns and scowls, some other body language that can discourage others and indicate guarded or hostile signals include crossed arms and legs, eye rolling, head shaking, and back turned toward the other person.[10]

Any time I've had to give a presentation in front of a large group, I have usually spotted both encouraging and discouraging body language coming from the listeners. I give a big thank you for all the encouragement that has come my way. Public speaking is difficult for me, and those positive vibes have always helped me make it through my talks.

During a clinical presentation I gave in pharmacy school, I spoke to our class and several faculty members. I was nervous and sweaty when I started. As I spoke, I locked in on a faculty member in the front row. She was leaning forward with her eyes wide open as if really interested in what I was saying. When I gave the clinical facts, she nodded repeatedly. Her encouraging body language was so comforting that it completely transformed me into a more relaxed and confident speaker. The encouragement made my presentation infinitely better. Even now, over twenty years later, I can still vividly picture that faculty member. Her body language cheered me on and prevented my total meltdown.

To get a good grasp on what encouragement looks like, watch cheerleaders. They have big smiles, lots of energy, and heads moving up and down as they shout, "We can do it!" and "Go team!" They face the crowd and engage them with open arms and wide eyes. If you bring such enthusiasm into your relationships, it will have an immediate, positive impact. I see it happen every day with people such as my wife and Sarah. When you encourage others in the midst of discouragement or hurt, you become much more than a cheerleader; you become God's cheerleader.

I feel very fortunate that I married one of God's cheerleaders. My wife, Mary Ann, has always found a positive spin to any problem we were facing and uses laughter and smiles to keep me from becoming upset or stressed. Anytime someone does something to intentionally or unintentionally upset me, she can laugh it off and keep me from becoming less than positive. When I hear her laugh or see her smile, I become happy and thankful for being with someone so special. Instead of arguing, she encourages. Instead of gossiping, she encourages. And instead of giving up, she encourages.

Encourage daily with sincere praise and compliments, generally and specifically. Thank and be thankful for everything. Speak with a positive vocabulary, tone, and body language.

Grow Spiritually through Encouragement

- Psalm 16:7: I will praise the Lord, who counsels me; even at night my heart instructs me.

- Psalm 7:17: I will give thanks to the Lord because of his righteousness; I will sing the praises of the name of the Lord Most High.

- Psalm 134:2: Lift up your hands in the sanctuary and praise the Lord.

- Ephesians 4:29: Do net let any unwholesome talk come out of your mouths, but only what is helpful for building others up according to their needs, that it may benefit those who listen.

chapter 2
quality time

Life is short. Don't miss opportunities to
spend time with people that you love.
-Joel Osteen

Two little girls played together on a farm in Nuyaka, Oklahoma, in 1960. There was no Internet, cable television, or smartphones to distract them. They had just their imaginations and boundless energy to play tag and patty-cake and engage in face-to-face conversation as they ate chocolate chip cookies outside on the front porch. One of the girls grew up to be the queen of country music with a tremendously successful career as a singer, songwriter, and actress. The other girl grew up to be the queen of our family—my mother.

I don't know if it's the good 'ol Southern hospitality or something about growing up on a farm, but those girls became women with a strong work ethic and deep passion for quality time with their families. My mother worked tirelessly as our family's breadwinner but always made me feel I was the priority in her life. When we had time together, the focus was on me and making our time of the utmost quality.

The queen of country I mentioned, Reba McEntire, shares the philosophy of not forgetting to make the time with your family count. In an *OK!* magazine interview, Reba had the following response to the question "Any advice on family?"

> I don't think quantity time is as special as quality time with your family. If I had to say the thing I regretted in my life, it's not spending enough time with my family. Then I look back and I think that the quality times were so special. I'm a big fan of that. I cherish the times we're all together. My son Shelby's like "Did you take pictures of anybody but me?" Ever since I was six months pregnant up to now. It's those special

times you spend with your family. Make time
for family.[11]

I believe my mother passed down to me my desire to make
the time we spend together as a family count. Whether it's with
my relatives, work family, or fraternity brothers and sisters, I've
always put a priority on the quality of time we spend together. I
liked it when the people around me were enjoying the moment,
and I often became stressed when that wasn't the case. Our time
on earth is limited, so we need to make the most of it.

> Why, you do not even know what will happen
> tomorrow. What is your life? You are a mist that
> appears for a little while and then vanishes.
> —James 4:14

The phrase *quality time* has been around since at least
the 70s[12] and has been steadily gaining popularity. Today,
quality time is a frequently cited term found in many business,
leadership, and relationship books and articles aimed at
teaching people how to make their time more productive and
meaningful. The definitions vary slightly, but they all have
a similar theme. Quality time is the time we invest our full,
focused, and uninterrupted attention in a person or a task.

While the catchphrase is relatively new, examples of people
engaging in quality time date to biblical times.

> After he had dismissed them, he went up on a mountainside
> by himself to pray. Later that night, he was there alone.
> —Matthew 14:23

Jesus didn't say, "Okay guys, peace out. I need to spend some one-on-one time with my main man God." But that's exactly what he did; he'd depart from his disciples, sometimes for days, to allow for fully focused, uninterrupted prayer with his Father.

Quality Time versus Quantity Time

A common misconception about quality time is that the amount of time spent has a direct correlation with the result, that more time with people equals better relationships just as more time on the driving range makes you a better golfer. Practice makes perfect, right? Wrong! *Perfect* practice makes perfect. Take it from someone who spent hours on the driving range only to go from bad to worse. It wasn't until I hired a pro to completely reshape my swing that I started to get better. He gave me knowledge and practice drills to improve my game.

Relationships are the same. It's takes more than simply spending quantities of time with someone to improve a relationship. And sadly, the more time we spend with certain people, the worse off our relationships with them can become.

We all have had bosses or crazy relatives we couldn't stand to be around. When we were forced to be in the same room with them, they inevitably did or said something that made us uncomfortable. Can you picture such people? If you can't, that person might be you!

Unfortunately, I have been this person on occasion. I used to think that as long as I was in the same room as my family, that counted as quality time. I would practice the guitar in the living room while my family was there watching television or playing games. I felt I was a great person for including my family in my personal time. I figured I could have been out golfing or doing any number of other things, but I was home. In my mind, this counted as great quality time. I couldn't have been more wrong.

The problem was that it usually started off on a good note (no pun intended) with me interacting with everyone. But it didn't take long for my focus to shift to my guitar, leaving my family frustrated and upset that they didn't have my attention. As my guitar practice became more difficult, it consumed more of my attention. My family had the expectation that I would be present physically and mentally, but after a few nonresponses to questions or responses that made no sense, they realized I had checked out.

I was hurting my relationship with my family. I would become noticeably frustrated at times when I was interrupted and therefore offered an even more-distant version of myself to them. The quantity of time was there, but the quality couldn't have been poorer. Not to mention the insanity I created by playing the first four bars to the same song over and over and over and over ...

Multitasking

Maybe I just needed to be better at multitasking, right? Unfortunately, no. This is another misconception about quality time. If quality time is heaven, multitasking is the well-intentioned path paved to you know where. Multitasking can rob our attention, cloud our focus, cause untimely interruptions, and dehumanize others by turning them into switches that are turned on and off without any regard for them. These effects create the opposite of quality time. And as the multiple tasks pile up and become more complex, it becomes stressful for everyone involved as the quality of interactions and task performance decline.[13]

But what if you're good at multitasking? If you're a good multitasker, raise your hand. If you just physically or mentally raised your hand, I have some bad news for you. A 2013 University of Utah study looked at how well people could multitask and found that participants who claimed to have above-average skills in multitasking often scored the lowest. The participants who claimed they rarely multitasked usually scored the highest.[14] What research such as this study has shown us is that we're all not quite as good at multitasking as we think we are. It also turns out that the people who multitask the most may be harming their short-term memory, creativity, IQ, and overall health.[15, 16, 17, 18]

Why is this? Well, it's true that we're all good at completing simple and automatic tasks seemingly simultaneously. I can jog and work my iPod for music and GPS feedback while monitoring my pace, heart rate, and surroundings pretty easily. I can fold towels and watch TV at the same time without mistakes. But when I try to juggle multiple tasks that become either too many in number or complexity, I begin to see the limitations and costs of multitasking.

One of the reasons why we start to struggle is because we really aren't doing things at exactly the same time but rather quickly switching back and forth between all the tasks.[19] Easy tasks such as folding towels take only fractions of a second; we can switch back and forth between folding and another task such as watching television. But if we're watching a breaking news broadcast telling us a nuclear bomb is headed for our neighborhood, we may just stop devoting attention to the towels and stare at the television like a statue.

This is because we're limited in the amount of attention we have to devote to our tasks since our attention is finite.[20] If something begins to dominate our attention, we'll have less available for anything else. It's like slicing a pie. Consider our attention as a pie; we have only so much attention we can cut into slices to handle the tasks we're facing. The more attention one requires, the bigger that slice becomes. If there are more hungry appetites than pie available, we'll run into problems—especially in our relationships.

The texting and driving epidemic illustrates the dangers of this concept. Driving requires nearly our full attention—most of our pie. We're piloting a two-thousand-pound projectile at high speeds. At sixty miles per hour, we travel eighty-eight feet per second. It takes only about four seconds—around the time it takes to read two sentences—to travel the length of a football field. And it takes only about one to two seconds not see an obstacle in front of us and crash, causing damage, injury and even death.

Juggling texting and driving at the same time cuts pieces of the driving pie. These small moments of not giving our full attention to the road cause accidents at an alarmingly increasing rate as more and more people text while driving. Phones recovered from fatal wrecks have been found with only two or three words typed. The people driving and texting may have thought they were doing both simultaneously, but the accidents prove otherwise.

The false sense that we are paying attention to both tasks at the same time creates what researchers have termed "inattentional blindness."[21] We miss out on much that is happening around us when we multitask. You think you have a clear path in front of you until that moment of impact. Bonk! A recent study found that 75 percent of people walking across a college campus while talking on their phones missed seeing a nearby clown on a unicycle.[22] Just imagine all the little things you could miss while multitasking your relationships.

Not only do we miss what others are doing; we also miss out on what we are doing ourselves, causing us to do things such as overeat or pour the whole bottle of syrup on our pancakes as we daze off in the distance thinking about something else. That's why when our attention is on our favorite television show, we can end up not realizing we just ate an entire bowl of popcorn or bag of chips.

I have frequently experienced this phenomenon when listening to a sports radio show while driving. Multitasking the driving and listening to the radio has often caused me to miss my exit. I have become so completely consumed with what they were saying that I easily lost track of my surroundings. The more attention I gave the radio, the less I gave to where I was. "Uh oh. I just missed my exit again."

Relationships are no different. If you continually try to multitask your way through them and don't give them your full attention, you can miss your turn and spend extra energy getting back on track or even wreck them. Have you ever been frustrated when someone started texting in the middle of a conversation and had no idea what you had just told them? Have you felt bad after asking someone to repeat something because you weren't paying attention? To have a positive, resonating effect on your relationships, give them your full attention and put the other tasks on hold.

The next problem with multitasking is that it clouds our focus. Shifting our focus from one task to another takes time and can decrease our productivity by as much as 40 percent.[23] We spend extra time completing the tasks, leaving less time for our relationships. That's because when we attempt to juggle tasks, it takes time to decide which task to switch to. It takes more time to make the switch. It takes even more time to warm up to the new task and get the wheels rolling again. All the time we spend switching our focus from one task to another is multiplied by the complexity of the tasks.[24] It may take a while to get back up to speed picking up where we left off from astrophysics problems after leaving orchestra composition and vice versa. But even simply talking on your phone while driving, which I don't recommend, has been shown to delay your arrival time.[25]

Another limitation we encounter while multitasking is that we are capable of holding only about five to nine things in our short-term memory at once.[26] We cannot focus on listening to a person telling us a story and read new information from, say, this eBook on a smartphone at the same time and get both streams of information to encode fully into our short-term memory. Without that short-term memory capture, there's no path for the information to be transferred to long-term memory for use later.[27] Engaging in other activities while trying to listen to others sets us up to forget the important details they told us.

Even after the information has made it into our long-term memory with all the other information we have stored up, we face another problem with multitasking that has to do with our actual brain design. Research has shown that the two hemispheres of our brains allow us to handle two complex situations at once as each hemisphere handles half the load.

But when we add a third complex task, we become literally overwhelmed, and that results in stress and the ultimate consequence of lost focus—mistakes.[28] Being overwhelmed, stressed out, and mistake prone is usually never good for our relationships.

Multitasking thus increases the likelihood of errors. I see this every day at the pharmacy; a big part of my job is to catch mistakes on prescriptions before they go out. And the number-one response I get when I call doctors' offices or ask my employees about errors on a prescription is, "I'm sorry. It was really busy." There was simply too much input to get good output. And the stress from making mistakes as well as the consequences of error can take a toll on your future abilities and damage the relationships involved.

What compounds the problem of dealing with too many tasks is our limitation of turning one task off completely as we move to another. As a pharmacist, I have made a majority of my mistakes when I've been unable to regain my focus as a result of multitasking in OHIO—not the state of Ohio but the state of mind when we **Only Handle It Once.** We aren't computers that can simply shut off our thinking about a certain task or situation once we decide to move on to another. Some situations have plagued me for entire days and made it difficult for me to focus on my job at all. For example, when a pharmacy customer threatened to attack me for not filling a pain medicine prescription, it put me in a fight-or flight-mode for several hours, and I found it difficult to refocus on my work. I constantly spent time thinking about what had been said, what exactly had gone wrong, my safety, my family's safety, and so on. I tried to refocus on my job, but those other thoughts came back to steal my focus and caused me to make mistakes.

This brings me to the next problem with multitasking: it causes interruptions. Multitasking continually interrupts the completion of one task for another, and nothing can steal attention and focus away faster than an interruption. That's why movie theaters show short commercials before the movie starts that ask people to turn off their phones. We all know it's difficult to focus on a movie when we're interrupted by the sounds of keyboard clicking or message notifications. If we are multitasking ourselves, it becomes even harder to tune out distractions.[29]

Unfortunately, we have little control over many of the interruptions that come our way, but we can manage them positively. And we never know when an unnecessary distraction can turn into a huge blessing. The problem with multitasking is that we often create our own interruptions that decrease our productivity and relational impact. We do things like watching television while studying for a test or playing smartphone games while someone is trying to converse with us over dinner. We can go to any restaurant today and find at least one couple staring at phones instead of each other.

I once tried to study for a pharmacy school final on a road trip to an OU/Texas football game 200 miles away. I thought I could study while attending the game. However, all I managed to do was ruin both events. I was unable to study in the car with my friends amid the infinite distractions and was unable to enjoy the game for fear of the test waiting like an angry samurai for my return. Each task interrupted the other by my own design.

The final and most important problem with multitasking is that tasks don't have feelings or expectations but people do. I've found most people don't like to be treated like switches that can be turned off and on. Trying to talk to someone scrolling through social media can be very frustrating. The continuous starting and stopping of a conversation and then repeating it is stressful. One study has shown that merely having a phone out in plain sight is enough to cause friction in a relationship.[30] Just the mere threat that you'll get multitasked and interrupted is often enough to do that.

Can you think of a time that you created problems while you were multitasking during your interactions with others? We all can. Our pastor once told us the story of how he tried to multitask working out at home while simultaneously participating on a conference call with a group of business and church leaders. He thought he could accomplish multiple tasks at once, but that attitude led to his forgetting to mute his phone after he spoke. The result was that all the conference call participants enjoyed his grunts and screams as he pushed his body to its exercise limits. The conference call participants began to ask what all the yells and screams were all about. Our pastor had some explaining to do.

I know we can't simply eliminate multitasking; we live in a multitasking world—companies pile on tasks for us to complete as we check our phone notifications between every breath. It would be impossible for me not to multitask as a pharmacist just as it would be impossible for my wife not to multitask at home. If she knocked out each task in order, she would finish preparing lunch before stopping little Jacob from cutting the dog's tail off, or keeping little Mason from "flying" off the top of the table, or answering little Meredith's question, "Can I have all this ice cream?" It would be terribly inefficient to sit in front of the washer and dryer until the loads were finished. I can't imagine someone just staring blankly at the clothes tumbling for two hours.

Multitasking is a skill that enables us to increase our efficiency at certain number of tasks of certain degrees of complexity but not without consequences. And there are cases where multitasking decreases efficiency. However, when we multitask in our relationships, the consequences can become magnified because, unlike tasks, people have expectations and feelings. To build positive relationships with people, it's better to do the opposite of multitasking and give them your full, focused, and uninterrupted attention—give them quality time.

Let's break down the components of quality time.

Full Attention

> I gave you my full attention…
> —Job 32:12

We must give our full attention, or the whole pie. Even if it lasts only one or two seconds, full attention can go a long way toward building and improving relationships. One of the quickest ways to show others they have our attention is with eye contact. When my children have felt they've lost my attention, they have pressed their foreheads against mine, forcing me to look directly into their eyes while asking, "Dad, what are you doing?" They are only kids, but they realize that if I'm watching TV or talking on the phone, I'm not giving them my full attention. When they are attempting to interact with me, receiving anything less than my full attention frustrates them.

Because God has blessed my wife and me with three fantastic, amazing children, I have had to be mindful of the amount of attention each one receives. I've routinely caught them each keeping a close watch on which one of them my eyes were focused on. I've had to divide the time equally so I didn't hurt any feelings. My wife also knows this. Just simply answering a phone call has set off an escalating, "Mom! *Mom! MOM!*" from our five-year-old as he attempted to deal with the fact that someone else had her full attention.

This frustration seems to be a common and natural reaction to losing someone's attention that I admittedly share with everyone else. When I see customers at the pharmacy become impatient while waiting for service, I use eye contact to keep the situation from getting out of hand. If I didn't make eye contact to let them know they had my attention, they would soon preform their own version of the "Mom! *Mom! MOM!*" routine. Just a few seconds of full attention can improve relationships and prevent problems.

When my wife and I attend our daughter's soccer or gymnastics practice; we think it's a great opportunity to spend quality time with her. We thought she would be a happier and better person knowing that her parents supported her. But unfortunately, we create problems by letting our attention wander. Meredith expects us to watch her play or practice, but when she sneaks a peek at us and sees us looking at our phones, talking to other parents, or playing with our other kids, she becomes disappointed. She'll quiz us on what happened during the practice to confirm our lack of attention. I learned that even when the practice or game is intense, she will inevitably look over for brief moments of eye contact. I do my best now to be ready and show her I'm paying full attention. When she sees we're paying attention, she tries harder and is happier on the ride home. The attention we give her increases the quality of her time on the field and with her family.

> We must pay the most careful attention, therefore, to
> what we have heard, so that we do not drift away.
> —Hebrews 2:1

If you want to give full attention, you need to pay attention. Paying attention to people's actions and body language has usually served me well. When I notice pharmacy customers in the drop-off line start to pace or tap their feet, I know they need a few seconds of full attention. Pick up any basic body language book to help you learn more about what people are saying. I put a few examples of some body language meanings in the "Understanding" chapter.

Paying attention to the words people use is also important. It's difficult if not impossible to have a meaningful conversation if you're not paying attention to the content. A head nod or an "uh huh" are ways you show you're listening but not necessarily paying full attention. Multitaskers can put these head nods on autopilot while concentrating on something else. I've gotten in trouble many times in the middle of a conversation when I was asked, "Are you even listening to me?" or "What did I just say?" I'd have no good answer. I was going along with the head nods and uh-huhs, but after too many in a row or a mistimed one, my lack of attention became apparent; I wasn't processing what I was hearing. So instead of getting into trouble, I try to add some meaningful dialog and engage in the conversation. That shows I'm paying full attention, and it keeps my mind from drifting off on a tangent. This will be discussed further under the "Listening" section in the "Understanding" chapter.

Giving and maintaining full attention is not always easy. In this busy, hectic world, many things will simultaneously compete for our attention. Some we cannot control, but others we can. It's possible to prevent ourselves from being our own worst enemies and maintaining full attention by dropping what we're doing to eliminate potential distractions. If we're reading and someone begins to talk to us, we should put down whatever we're reading before we respond—drop it! Such an act is a powerful quality time component and relationship builder.

A group of our friends and family were watching my alma mater, the University of Oklahoma, play for the NCAA college football championship at a house party hosted by Curt, a good friend of mine. When the game was close and we were all on the edge of our seats, one of Curt's sons asked a question, and Curt muted the television! He turned to face his son before answering. I thought, *Wow! That's a huge display of full attention.* Curt put the party on hold to give his son a moment of quality time.

I'm often guilty of letting minor distractions compete for and often dominate my attention, leaving a trail of frustrated and disappointed people. Many times, my wife has been talking to me while we're driving, and she thinks I'm listening and processing the information. When she hears me laugh at a comment on a sports radio show, however, she realizes where my attention has been. I can see the sadness on her face, and I feel terrible. I've learned to take a page out of Curt's playbook and mute the sports show when she's talking to me or not turn it on in the first place. That increases our quality time in the car.

And please, put the phones down! It seems as if we're all turning into smartphone zombies who have forgotten how to have face-to-face conversations. It's sad that our real conversations are becoming the distractions to our phone time.

I see the old becoming just as guilty as the young. Once, I was behind an older woman picking up a take-out meal. As the restaurant employee was attempting to review her large order, all she could do was stare at her phone while scrolling though about a hundred status updates. There was no way she could have possibly been processing the information on her phone because of how fast those fingers were sliding up and down the screen. It was obvious to everyone behind her in line that she wasn't paying attention to the employee. Forgive me, Lord (I know I need spiritual help in this area), but I was really hoping that her meal was accidentally left out of the big order and she wouldn't realize it until she got home. We all need to get back to the times when the people in front of us got our full attention.

Focused Time

Quality time is focused time. The focus can be on people or tasks, but it must be shared by everyone involved to count. This is why you can't force quality time on someone. You can force someone to be with you with full attention, but if the focus isn't shared (if they're focused on getting away and your focus is on making them stay), that's not quality time. I doubt the captor really has the captive's full attention anyway; the captive is probably thinking, *Please Lord, help me get out of here.*

When we're dating and things are going well, we can have quality times enjoying dinner, seeing a movie, and mutually engaging good conversation. This can also happen in the workplace when people spend time together to complete tasks. This is one contributor to how workplace relationships occur.

Working everyday with someone can give us occasions of quality time, a positive relational builder that leads to a strong relational bond.

This shared focus phenomenon can explain why people who play on sports teams can have strong relationships with one another. The teammates create quality time as they intensely focus on the team's goals. This could also explain why if one of the teammates doesn't share the same goals and starts to focus on personal goals, the relationships decline. The team goals and the personal goals don't mesh, so no quality time is created, and the potential to enhance relationships is lost.

When my pharmacy interns are about to interview for positions with our company, I help them prepare by letting them know what the interviewers will focus on. My supervisors make it clear to me which metrics and services we are accountable for are at the top of the list, so I prepare my interns to have good discussions about those key topics. This technique has led to positive, resonating dialog during their interviews. The resonating effects have continued well after, when the hiring manager later excitedly tells me about the great time they had with the candidates.

Another way to use shared focus to create quality time is by learning about others' hobbies and interests. Talking about these topics can cast an interaction in a positive light. Even on my most stressful days, if someone asks me how my kids are doing, I can't help but shift my thinking to them as I answer. This focus shift always puts me in a good mood; I stop worrying about whatever was stressing me out and start thinking about spending more time with my family.

When I meet new people, I often try to learn as much as I can about what activities they spend their extra time doing.

Sometimes, I have even tried the activities out for myself to get a better understanding so we could discuss their interests in more detail. I learned a lot about the Bible as I used this approach with my coworker Sarah. She definitely walks the spiritual walk, so I had a rich resource and example to learn from. I would ask her, "What did you talk about in church this week?" Sarah's life revolves around church, so discussing the Bible and what we learned at church made our time at work together richer. Also, I began to really become interested in the Word and how it applies to our lives, and that created a win-win situation.

Knowing that you can share the focus of a task with someone creates an infinite number of potential quality time moments that don't have to be planned. Doing the dishes or folding the laundry with someone are quick and easy quality time moments and powerful relationship builders. Those small amounts of time can resonate well after the event is over.

When my three- and five-year-old sons are playing in the bathtub, I may just unexpectedly throw on a pair of shorts and jump in there with them and play whatever silly game they have underway. I know we had a quality time experience when they enthusiastically ask me to join them again and again.

At the pharmacy, I get visits from my supervisor about once a month as long as things are going well. I've had several supervisors during my pharmacy career. When most of them would come into our store and see that we were busy or behind schedule, they would nonetheless tell me my shelves were too dusty, I needed to work harder with fewer resources, and so on. But only a couple of my bosses literally rolled up their sleeves and worked by my side to get me caught up with my tasks before they relayed the company information I needed. Working with those managers was quality time that made our whole pharmacy staff more receptive to their feedback and direction. And even though they're no longer my direct supervisors, I still have a positive, resonating relationship with them.

That's why it's also important to plan for quality time. When I became the president of my pharmacy school fraternity, I struggled to get members to attend our chapter meetings. When I started to get increased attendance, I had problems keeping them focused on what I had to say. Everyone, including myself, was having a less than good time. I knew I could do much better.

I realized I needed to switch the focus of the meetings. I decided to make the meetings fun. I planned TV show-like games with cheap prizes for winners and consequences for losers, including pies in the face. Before long, attendance and participation were at all-time highs. The group enjoyed having fun, and that created great quality time. Right before the meetings would end, I would get their full attention and spend a few minutes getting our business information out. Our chapter began to perform so well that we received national attention and visit from the fraternity CEO, who lived half way across the country.

There is science behind my fraternity success. When you get a workgroup laughing and having fun, it contagiously connects them on a primal level; the group becomes engaged and productive.[31] Good speakers frequently start their talks and presentations with ice-breaker jokes and inject humor into their presentations to connect with the audience. After I got the group connected with games, they were willing to do the fraternity work. Presto!

The formula worked so well that I took the philosophy with me into my professional career. At first, I was worried that maybe I wasn't maturing correctly and that I shouldn't be having fun at work. I was criticized by a few managers early on who tried to discourage me from having a good time on the clock. Then I received the assignment of reading *NUTS!* by Herb Kelleher, former CEO of Southwest Airlines. While all other airlines were going bankrupt, Southwest was making a profit. One of the many great things Herb did was encouraging a culture of fun at work.[32] As a result, Southwest had the most productive employees. Yes, the responsibility of getting passengers 30,000 feet up and down is serious, but that doesn't mean you can't laugh and have a good time while you do it. That's all I needed to know! From then on, I was a Herb Kelleher disciple, and having fun was always going to be one of my priorities.

Having a good time at work is also effective because it can create quality time. Since most people like to have fun, it makes sense that this is an easily shared goal to plan for. Once everyone is sharing in a fun experience, you can create quality time and build relationships. It quickly creates a situation in which everyone wants to do his or her best not necessarily for the organization but rather for one another. Customers have told me they can feel the love in our pharmacy. A week doesn't go by without a random customer telling us that it looks like we're having too much fun back there. That's one of the greatest compliments I could get because that means we're having quality time. Productivity naturally rises as a result, and the company benefits.

Sometimes, I plan for quality time, but it all goes wrong as soon as the fun goes away and the focus changes. The first golf lesson I gave my daughter was less than optimal. I was a rookie instructor who made things extremely difficult and stressful for her. I could tell she wasn't having a good time; whatever enthusiasm she had for golf was left behind at the range. After we got home, I asked her if there was anything she still liked about golf. She told me it was a lot of fun driving the cart. So sometime later, when we gave it another try, it went infinitely better because we made it fun. I let her drive the cart all over the place before and after hitting balls. We used a mat so striking the ball became much easier, and she made a ton of great shots! We were smiling and laughing throughout the entire experience, and her attitude and performance improved. She asked to do it again. That's the difference fun makes! I hope Herb would be proud.

The last area of focus that can greatly hamper or enhance quality time is attitude. Fun usually leads to a good attitude, but sometimes, you just need to already have it. My daughter once told me, "Dad, attitude is a little thing that makes a big difference." Was she ever right! One hot summer morning, our three kids asked, "What are we going to do today?" Mom came up with the idea of playing in the sprinklers in the backyard. Two of our kids cheered while one sat with crossed arms and a negative demeanor until noticing all the fun everyone else was having and joined in, albeit reluctantly and unenthusiastically. But before you knew it, a scowl turned into a beaming smile, and all three kids were having great quality time.

We have all at one time or another gone into situations with our arms crossed and an "I don't want to" attitude on our faces. I avoided fishing trips; I was squeamish when it came to slimy fish and frogs that have microorganisms all over them. I let my microbiology lab memories of what the world looked like under a microscope sideline me. I avoided countless fishing trips over the years until I finally ran out of excuses.

I went on a camping trip with my family with plans to fish for maybe a few hours one day. I thought I could easily get through it by putting fake rubber fishing lures on the kids' lines. The problem was that another couple on the trip wanted to use live bait. So there I was, digging into cans of live worms and hooking them up for my children. I didn't want to do it, but I wasn't going to let my attitude create any drama. I also wanted to set a good example for my children watching. So I dove in.

A couple of hours of fishing turned into fishing all day, then every day of the trip. By the end of the trip, I realized I enjoyed fishing with my family. I even purchased some new fishing gear and planned to do it again.

I've learned that whether it's a business meeting, a trip to the supermarket, or even something I might think will turn into my worst nightmare, I should uncross my arms and run through the sprinkler. Focusing on a good attitude can change a bad event into a great quality time moment.

Uninterrupted

Nothing decreases focus and attention quicker than interruptions. A doorbell ringing during dinner, a phone going off in a theater, a dog barking while you're reading a book—so many interruptions can create frustration and anxiety and hamper quality time. But do they have to?

At work, when I'm checking prescriptions, the phone can become a huge interruption for me. When the ringing ceases, I go back to being productive; I rarely have to double or triple check anything. However, I just can't turn the phones off; I wouldn't want to deny people my help because I happen to be checking a prescription when they call. At the same time, I don't want to put the patient whose prescription I'm checking at risk. I have my staff help me by answering the phones quickly or putting calls on hold if I'm in the middle of checking a prescription. It's all about managing interruptions.

But what if you wanted some quality time by yourself and sat on a park bench to read something and were interrupted by a stranger who asked, "How are you doing?" How would you manage that interruption?

Mark 5 tells the story of Jesus and his disciples being interrupted when they were on an urgent mission to save the daughter of a ruler of the synagogue. When Jesus stopped to help a woman who had been unable to participate in community life for twelve years, his disciples became frustrated. As a result of the interruption, the ruler's daughter died. But the delay created an even greater experience than could have been achieved by Jesus' simply healing the daughter; he performed an even greater miracle by bringing her back from the dead. And he had helped someone else along the way.

It's easy to become frustrated with interruptions as the disciples were. While you can always move to another "bench," I suggest you at least engage in short conversations with the strangers you come across because you never know what kind of blessing interruptions can turn out to be. I'm learning to take a page out of the book *Interrupted* by Jen Hatmaker and embracing life's interruptions, planned and unplanned, to create a better story. I'm learning to let God take the lead and not see unexpected events as unwanted changes but rather as new beginnings and opportunities.

God does not change, but he uses change to
change us. He sends us on journeys that bring
us to the end of ourselves. We often feel out of
control, yet if we embrace His leading, we may
find ourselves on the ride of our lives.[33]
—Jen Hatmaker

One night, I was driving with my family to a restaurant
when my phone rang. The only time my phone rings is when
a telemarketer is dying to tell me about an amazing deal only
I "qualify" for. Uncharacteristically, instead of eliminating
the interruption by hitting the end call button, I managed the
interruption by asking my wife to answer it. It turned out to be
a representative of the company that eventually published this
book. I informed the representative about my current situation
in the car and said I'd contact her later that night. I had quality
time with my family that evening and began a relationship with
the publisher the following day. That interruption turned into
a huge blessing!

With technology allowing everyone to have access to us
twenty-four hours a day 365 days a year and social media
putting us on notification overload, interruptions are just part
of life. It's how we manage them that makes the difference.
Some we can control, but others we can't. When we eliminate
unnecessary distractions and manage interruptions, that can
allow us to give our full attention to creating and maintaining
quality time.

Growing Spiritually through Quality Time

- James 4:14: Why, you do not even know what will happen tomorrow. What is your life? You are a mist that appears for a little while and then vanishes.

- Ephesians 5:15–16: Be very careful, then, how you live—not as unwise but as wise, making the most of every opportunity, because the days are evil.

- Psalm 1:2: But whose delight is in the law of the Lord, and who meditates on his law day and night.

- Matthew 6:6: But when you pray, go into your room, close the door and pray to your Father, who is unseen. Then your Father, who sees what is done in secret, will reward you.

chapter 3
understanding

E
Q
U
I
P

Understanding can overcome any situation, however
mysterious or insurmountable it may appear to be.
—Norman Vincent Peale

It was a usual weekend for my son Mason. He was the first one up on Saturday morning to get ready for his soccer game. As he put on his little cleats, he excitedly said, "I'll score some goals today and get another medal!"

In his league, they awarded a medal each week to an outstanding player, and Mason had already racked up two of them. The first one was after his debut as a soccer player. He was a natural. It was fall, and many of the games were played in cold, wet, windy weather. While a lot of the other five-year-old and under kids complained or refused to play, Mason was one of the first players to run out excitedly on the field. He had a true passion for the game and played aggressive offense and tenacious defense. Many times, the kids on the opposing team became frustrated with Mason's defense and unsuccessfully tried to push him down. And my son's offensive skills once got him six goals in a single game.

After the game was over, we dropped Mason off at his Mee Maw's for a day of running around and jumping on the trampoline with his uncle, brother, and sister. We picked him up on Sunday, and it was off to church, where he engaged in his favorite activity—playing on the monkey bars with the kids in his Sunday school class. After church, we went out for pizza and enjoyed a fun time together.

When we got home, Mason's laughter turned to silence. Mason told me that his hip hurt and that he had a leg injury. I told him to shake it off and go to bed. He seemed okay, so I didn't worry. I thought he probably had overdone it with a full weekend of activity. But in the middle of the night, he woke us up complaining of severe hip pain. We knew something was wrong and took him to the doctor the next day. That turned into an X-ray, another X-ray, and an appointment with a children's orthopedic specialist.

Unfortunately, that's when we found out that our little angel had Perthes disease, a condition that interrupts the blood supply to the bone at the top of the leg. The ball that fits into his hip socket was disintegrating. The specialist told us that for the next couple of years, Mason couldn't run, jump, or even walk long distances until the disease ran its course, at which point, we might have to put him in a cast and brace for another year or two and even possibly have to have him undergo a hip replacement down the road. That news meant no more recess, PE, soccer, monkey bars, trampoline, or hiking—all the things Mason loved and lived for.

How do you make a child understand he can't play like other kids for the next few years and possibly forever? How do you show understanding to the parents who have to watch their innocent child be robbed of a good portion of his childhood? How can you understand what it's like to pull into the garage and see Mason's tiny cleats on a shelf and know he won't be playing the game he loved for a long time?

I'd never experienced the intensity of emotions that go along with this kind of diagnosis; showing understanding to me can definitely be a slippery slope. I know many people had good intentions when they made comments to my wife and me about Mason, but many times, their comments made us angry, upset, and even hostile on occasion.

However, two people stood out as the ones who were able to deeply connect with us when showing their understanding: James, who wept with us when he brought Mason a Lego set his son had picked out, and a church member with a disabled child who reached out to my wife with a message.

One night, my wife came to me with tears running down her face. She showed me a text a church member had sent her. It was so powerful and moving that it immediately made us feel better about the whole situation. It didn't solve our problems, but it made them solvable. It guided our path and told us others cared; it built a strong relationship that resonated trust, courage, and openness; and it didn't simplify or make light of the situation or offer solutions. Right when we were lost and worried about the future, her example of understanding gave us hope. She wrote,

> Of all the women in the world, God chose you to be Mason's mom because He knew you are what Mason needs. God has already equipped you for this task. You will have days where you feel overwhelmed and underequipped and wish God had chosen someone else. I can name women who can do a better job than me, but God chose me. Mason doesn't need someone else, he needs you. Take your time and grieve the diagnosis. Then when you're done, dry your face and just take one step at a time. In the beginning, there were more days I spent crying than walking, but it gets better with time. Now, I walk more than I cry, but I'm not ashamed to admit I still cry sometimes and wish a different life for my boys.

That's how you show understanding!

Sometimes, people have asked me what was the most important component of the EQUIP model. While I feel they work together like the strings of a guitar, if I had to narrow it down to one, I would go with understanding. Without it, your other efforts could be mistimed or misguided and create more problems for you and your relationships. In my most difficult relationships, I've had to first get an understanding before I could make any progress and open the door for the other EQUIP components.

Stephen Covey's *The 7 Habits of Highly Effective People* includes habit 5: Seek first to understand then to be understood.[34] I read this book in pharmacy school, and it's been a major influence in my life since. It has taught me many lessons, including the importance of understanding.

Covey's book was again part of my curriculum a few years later in my MBA program; it taught me just how important things such as understanding are in all aspects of life. And still today, how to relationally understand others is being taught in many classrooms across all occupations with an emphasis on properly *showing* understanding.

Just having a good understanding of a situation will not help if you fail to show your understanding in a way that makes a positive impact. You may understand someone is sad and grieving the loss of a close relative, but that alone won't do anything for the relationship if you say something offensive such as, "Better him than you!" or "She shouldn't have been out that day" or "I bet you can't wait to spend all that insurance money."

During an empathy lecture at the same college of pharmacy I attended nearly twenty years ago, the professor asked the class to share an example of when someone showed them some understanding. An intern of mine, told about arriving at work after a long day in the midst of a rough week in a trying season. Her boss noticed she was stressed and asked her if everything was okay. She expelled a deep breath and explained, in a somewhat irritated tone, that she was having an impossible time juggling all her responsibilities and that everything in her life was piling up. Her boss told her that he realized she had a tough life attending class, working, socializing, and being a single mom of three and that he understood she was under a lot of stress. She said those words from her boss transformed her mood immediately. As soon as she realized someone else understood her situation, she felt everything was much better and she'd be okay. She wasn't looking for sympathy, pity, solutions, or a fairy-tale ending; she was looking for understanding. Once she got it, she went from upset and stressed back to normal and productive. She had new life.

The Bible includes one of the greatest examples of understanding. It gave us the famous and commonly cited phrase used today as a metaphor for judging others: "Let's not throw stones." It comes from John's recording of an angry mob about to stone an adulterer. What stopped the execution? Understanding. Jesus told the mob that whoever among them was without sin could throw the first stone. (John 8:7) If one stone had been thrown, that would have prompted a barrage of stones. Unfortunately, that was not an uncommon practice in those times. But instead of acting, each person in the mob was forced to think about his or her personal issues and battles with sin. They were all asked to understand that they had all fallen short at times and that even though the adulterous woman was a sinner, so were they. No stones were thrown. A life was saved. That's the power of understanding.

The more I understand myself and others, the more I realize we're so much alike. We share many of the same basic needs, wants, and desires, and that can lead to the same issues, problems, and conflicts. When a person tries to communicate with another, he or she does so to fulfill a need. We send a message coded in the form of body language, tone, and content.[35] The receiver of the code attempts to decipher it to form an understanding of the meaning. If the message is misunderstood, problems can result. But when the meaning of the code is uncovered, the listener gains understanding.

We don't have to fulfill the need or solve the problem, but we should demonstrate our understanding to the person who originated the message to positively affect the relationship. However, until the correct understanding is confirmed, any action may be premature or misguided. It may become evident that the person's only need was for someone to simply acknowledge his or her situation. While the process may require a lot of work at times, it's well worth the investment. Just like the adulterous woman, I've yet to meet anyone who couldn't benefit from a little understanding.

Yet here we are over 2,000 years later still putting up barriers and blocking our attempts to understand others. Here's an example of a time when I failed to show understanding to my wife, and it had a negative effect on our relationship. Once, I thought I knew how my wife was feeling or should be feeling about the challenges of being a stay-at-home mom. She frequently tried to express her frustrations; she was looking for a little bit of acknowledgment and encouragement to keep pushing on. Instead, I did the opposite. My lack of understanding was very discouraging to her and put a strain on our marriage. I was a fool.

Fools find no pleasure in understanding, but
delight in airing their own opinions.
—Proverbs 18:2

When she told me how stressful it was to clean up a room just to have it turned into a complete mess in three seconds, I would throw a stone and tell her, "At least you don't have to go to a job every day and deal with bosses, upset customers, corporate red tape, and all that kind of stress." To which she replied, "I wish sometimes I did have a regular job to go to so I could at least have an adult conversation and talk about something besides SpongeBob."

I didn't even acknowledge the frustration caused by her seeing her efforts as futile or the lack of opportunities to interact and converse with adults daily—I just didn't get it.

It gets worse. I would think she was ungrateful; *How could she not be happy with her stay-at-home mom role I've so graciously provided her? She was the one who wanted to be a stay-at-home mom.* I explained how good she had it, what a blessing it was for her to be able to stay with the kids, and that some stay-at-home moms had more than three kids. I was the angry mob. I was composed of an angry idiot, angry jerk, and an angry insensitive guy all wrapped in one and holding a bucketful of opinionated stones to throw.

My wife thought, *Okay, game on!* She came up with a plan. On my day off, she left our three children with me for several hours while she ran errands. When she came home (she said she had been gone for just a few hours, but I felt it was a couple of months), I was shivering in the corner of a destroyed house waving a white flag. The children had defeated me about five minutes after she had left. The constant questions, demands for food and entertainment, diapers, messes and near-fatal accidents gave me a whole new perspective on what my poor wife was going through every day. I was unable to get anything accomplished other than keeping us all alive until she got back. I was physically and mentally exhausted.

I learned that being a stay-at-home parent is a tough task and that it was a huge blessing for me my wife was able and willing to accept the challenge and sacrifice many of her personal goals. I finally gained understanding. I hugged her, apologized, and changed my schedule so I'd be available to help out more. Final score: Mary Ann 35, Me 0.

It took me experiencing the situation of being a stay-at-home parent to gain that understanding. Going through a similar experience or walking in another's shoes can definitely be the best teacher of understanding, but it would be impossible for us to experience everything others go through to accomplish that. Even when we do have similar experiences to draw on, we can still have different perspectives. One might see the cup as half full while another sees it as half empty. Even when we do share the same understanding, we still have to show that. I suggest following a step-by-step approach that can lead to showing understanding whether you have experience or not with a situation.

Pathway to Showing Understanding in Relationships

Here is how I believe the pathway to showing understanding in relationships flows. It starts with a person in a situation expressing a need and ends with someone else receiving the information, processing the information, and showing his or her understanding back to the person. The pathway to understanding is simple and straightforward, but much can go wrong along the way as we hit barriers, detours, or roadblocks. The process requires knowledge, effort, and discipline to make it to the end and show our understanding to the other. But the positive effect it makes on relationships is well worth it.

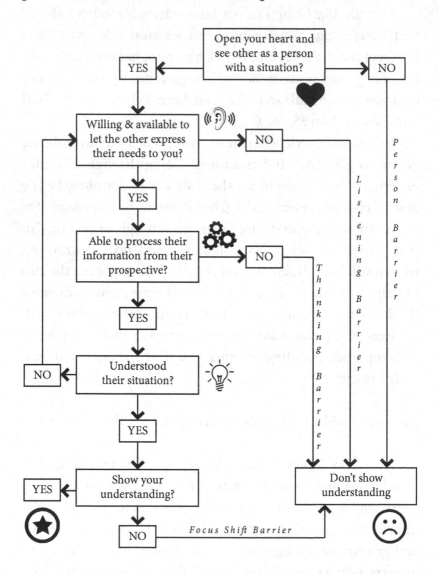

Those in the angry mob had a bias barrier, a judgmental attitude that prevented them from getting to the showing understanding point. In their minds, they had already held a trial, judged the woman, and sentenced her to death. They failed to see the woman as a person dealing with a problem and in need of help. Instead, blind to their own sins, they saw her as someone who deserved the ultimate physical punishment.

Before I go over the ways to help us show understanding, let's take a look at some of the common problems, such as judging, that prevent us from getting there.

Let the Lord judge the peoples...
—Psalm 7:8

Barriers to Understanding

Person Barriers

"This idiot has no idea how to drive."
"That's what happens when you're a liar."
"They look terrible because they're lazy."
"They're homeless because they refuse to work for a living."

The first problem comes when we stop seeing people as individuals dealing with life situations and start seeing them as stereotypical members of a group. In the previous example of the stay-at-home mom, I had an issue with the person part of the pathway when I changed my wife from a person with frustrations into a "typical" stay-at-home parent. I thought that role was difficult at times but overall much easier than being in the workforce. I assumed I knew everything about it. Therefore, I was refusing to take in and process any new information.

A bias is a mental tendency, especially an irrational preference or prejudice. It's also a diagonal cut across the weave of a fabric.[36] Both definitions apply. Not only did I have irrational ideas of how easy stay-at-home parents had it, but I also took a short "cut" through the process of receiving and processing information and showing understanding. I missed steps in the pathway and defaulted straight to my prejudices. Of course I thought workforce people such as myself had it much harder than stay-at-home moms just as the angry mob thought they were holier than the sinning woman. The result was that I threw an opinion stone instead of seeking and then showing understanding.

What's worse is that the unveiling of my prejudice potentially created a twofold problem that stifled any chance of future understanding. Since once I had made it clear that I wasn't willing to take in any new information about my wife's needs and that I had already placed her in the ungrateful, stay-at-home mom category, my wife became less likely to express her needs to me. So both sides shut down communication. This is why kids often don't want to talk to adults or parents about sex, drugs, or rock 'n' roll because they're sure they know what their parents will have to say. Once your sons and daughters know your judgment, they have little reason to ask the question[37]; they feel that you just won't understand their take on the matter.

Ironically, I'm very familiar with barriers such as biases and even studied them in pharmacy school when we learned how to critically think about clinical data. For example, companies that have a vested interest in the results of a study they sponsor might show only data that favors their interests. Yet I still allowed bias to corrupt my thinking and have frequently caught myself doing it on several occasions.

We're all guilty at times of consciously leaving out facts from our complaints that don't favor our sides; that seems to be natural and common. Sometimes, we consciously do it, but other times, it's unconscious. Such biases can be sneaky and even programmed into us.

I recently watched an experiment in which young children were asked to run, punch, and fight like a girl. All the children looked like little superheroes bursting with strength, dexterity, and confidence. Then, adults were asked to do the same, and they portrayed weak, uncoordinated, and insecure gestures, having developed irrational stereotypes of the female gender.[38] Why the difference between the kids' and the adults' answers? Society can create these weak stereotypes and reinforce them through culture and media, and generations pass them down. I know this to be true; I was given the assignment of watching the experiment by my wife after I had made a negative stereotypical comment to our daughter in the presence of her two younger brothers. I had reinforced a bias.

My father always taught me that women were just as good at things as men were, and I believe that. One of my favorite athletes on many levels is Bethany Hamilton, who didn't let a shark attack resulting in the loss of her arm stop her from dominating the waves on her surfboard. Yet I still jokingly made a "Women are inferior at hunting and fishing" comment to my daughter. I'm thankful my wife was smart enough and strong enough to nip that in the bud.

> Courage, sacrifice, determination, commitment,
> toughness, heart, talent, guts. That's what little
> girls are made of.
> —Bethany Hamilton

I've caught myself being irrationally prejudiced against people even at work. I like my profession; it affords me the chance to help so many people every day. But I unfortunately developed a lack of understanding for a specific group of patients based on several bad experiences. It's not fair and certainly not scientifically sound to be prejudiced against new patients with similar conditions. Everyone is unique and has a unique set of circumstances.

The problem I had was with people who would attempt to get early refills for pain medications; I thought they were manipulating the health care system to get pain meds and I'd judge them accordingly. Though they would explain their frustrations with the pain and how their therapy wasn't working, I had already convicted them as guilty of trying to scam me, and I showed them little understanding.

That was until I experienced several months of chronic back pain. I followed all the doctors' protocols to a T and even went through three months of physical therapy, but I still wasn't healing completely. Usually, over-the-counter anti-inflammatories gave me enough relief to get me through standing all day at work, but on a few occasions, nothing would relieve the pain. I had great difficulty concentrating on anything and wondered how I could continue to be a pharmacist in that condition. Once again, the experience gave me a new understanding for my back pain patients against whom I had once been biased and was finally able to show them understanding.

It's funny how I'm slow to realize a bias toward someone else but fast to recognize when others have a bias toward me. When I was a pharmaceutical sales rep, I found that some doctors had a negative bias toward salespeople that prevented them from receiving my information and therefore threw up roadblocks. I felt those doctors believed most salespeople and their companies would say anything to get them to prescribe their drugs. I was foolish to think that my doctorate of pharmacy degree would prevent them from thinking that about me and that I might have more credibility. In fact, the degree may have hindered me in the beginning.

During the first week in my territory, I was called a sellout by one doc, and another told me I could get a cup of coffee with fifty cents and my degree in pharmacy. There I was, trying to get my information out to people who wouldn't receive it. Instead of showing me any understanding, they showed me sarcasm, little patience, and the exit door.

I quickly realized that I had to remove this bias barrier before the information could have a chance to get out and be understood. I could have just thrown my hands up, following the "My parents just don't understand" mind-set and told myself they would never understand me anyway, so why try? I could have continued to pound away with an ineffective approach to deaf ears. But neither of those strategies would do much for my sales quotas or the relationships I was trying to develop with those doctors. I needed to get them to stop seeing me as a salesperson and start seeing me as Doug, a person doing his job of delivering my company's information.

So over the next several visits, I didn't bring up any sales information; instead, I tried to become a resource that would answer all questions about my drug as well as those of the competition's. It didn't take long before questions started to trickle in. Most of the doctors had questions about our drug's higher price, but after I gave several honest answers, I was able to get past the bias blockade and get them to listen to me promote our drug's benefits.

But there were still some doctors who stonewalled me; some wouldn't even see me. How do you make such people understand you? Just as you can't force quality time on people, you can't force understanding on them. But there are still options. When it comes to dealing with those who resist any communication and thus any chance to achieve understanding, I've found it helpful to enlist the help of others such as peers, mediators, or counselors. Jesus, the ultimate counselor, stepped in and communicated to the angry mob to help them achieve understanding. In the case of the doctors, I would try to get them to meet with a group of their peers over lunch or dinner to discuss the pros and cons of our drug. This method circumvented the barrier and gave me a greater chance to have my message of potential benefits received, processed, and understood.

And it worked! Our territory sales increased so much that it raised our entire district two spots up the company charts.

Listening Barriers

"I can't even hear this guy."
"You're crazy if you think it's my fault!"
"I'm so confused."
"Will this story ever end?"
"I wonder if those jeans are still on sale. Wait! Maybe I should buy cords. Hmmm. But what color?"

The next phase in the pathway to showing understanding deals with the actual information given to us to decipher. The first step in receiving this information is listening to it, not just simply hearing it. Studies show that listening is the most used communication skill by people; it beats out reading, writing, and speaking. But when they measure how well people listen, they find most people score poorly.[39] We're able to retain only half of what we hear immediately after a ten-minute presentation, and two days later, we can recall only a fourth of the information. Why are we so bad at something so important?

One reason is because we get little training in listening. We can all remember getting plenty of reading and writing lessons in school with the occasional oral presentation thrown in, but how many listening lessons did we have? I can remember only one, from seventh grade. We had a guest speaker play the old telephone game. She had a volunteer wear headphones while she told the rest of the class a short story. She had one of us who had heard the story go out in the hallway and tell the story to the student who'd had earphones on, and that student retold the story to the class. It was clear that the new storyteller had most of the details incorrect and hadn't heard others.

We do the same thing in our relationships. I usually can't remember someone's name five minutes after being introduced to him or her. To make things worse, our listening skills can decline with age.[40] It's no surprise that as adults, we think we have an understanding of something, but in reality, we grasp only a fraction of the information coming our way, leaving the rest misunderstood.

Another big contributor to our problems with listening is that we listen about four times faster than we speak.[41] Therefore, as we listen, we're using only 25 percent of our mental capacity, leaving 75 percent to drift off or go off on tangents. It's almost effortless and natural to let these barriers give us a false understanding. It's much easier to quickly tell ourselves, *Oh, I got it*, and miss some important details. When it comes to understanding, the details are everything.

Even if you become a great listener, you can still encounter problems with the actual information being conveyed. For example, information that is confusing, too loud, too quiet, too much, or too little can create problems. One of my great mentors once told me to always keep business e-mails short and sweet by keeping them to two or three paragraphs of two to three sentences each. That will keep readers from being overwhelmed with information and increase the chances of your e-mail being read and understood. I receive several business e-mails daily from our corporate office, my direct supervisors, and others. I usually skip the lengthy ones or skim through them at best. My wife will not even forward me a lengthy joke e-mail, because she knows I'll probably not read it. I'm simply bombarded with information e-mails daily, so the shorter ones get my best look.

I see the same phenomenon with personal stories. When someone is giving you a long-winded saga with a lot of side stories and tangential information, it's hard to stay focused, make it to the end, and understand the point of the story. Of course, I encourage all listeners to make an effort, but the more information they have to deal with, the harder it is to understand. It can at times become overwhelming trying to keep up while worrying about when the tale will end. We can get so caught up in the details and information of the side stories that the main intention gets overlooked or is difficult to discern.

Sometimes, patients will come into the pharmacy with a newly diagnosed condition such as diabetes. These patents have usually just received a crash course in their medical condition, the drug therapy to remedy it, and the medical devices used to monitor it. By the time they make it to the pharmacy to drop off their prescriptions, they have that deer-in-the-headlights expression and little to no understanding of the information they received at the doctor's office. I can tell they're overwhelmed, and that presents me with a great opportunity to help them make sense of everything. Unfortunately, I have the opposite problem of often not providing enough information and then becoming frustrated that the patient doesn't understand what I'm trying to convey.

Once, my wife and I went to a mall to return an ill-fitting pair of pants I had bought online from Gap; I simply wanted to exchange them for the correct size. I looked for the pants and asked an employee to check the backroom. I realized it wasn't going to be an easy exchange. After an employee kindly and professionally exhausted every resource, I learned I would have to simply accept a refund and reorder online. I spent around twenty minutes going through several steps before I got the answer. I didn't want to reorder online and wait for them. I was frustrated. I stormed over to my wife, who was peacefully browsing some items. When I told her, "Let's go!" while holding nothing in my hands, she looked puzzled. She asked, "What about the pants?" In a caveman-like response, I said something like, "Don't have ... Refund ... Reorder." She stared at me blankly while trying to make sense of my ramblings. The fact that she didn't understand me increased my frustration even though I had given her way too little information. It was crazy for me to expect her to understand in three seconds what had taken me twenty minutes to experience. So now, anytime I give her too little information, she jokingly asks if I'm trying to "Gap pants" her.

This brings up an interesting point about my view that people are either condensers or expanders of information. Condensers such as myself prefer to reduce the relevant information to simple sentences or bullet points; we want to know just the point of the story and the bottom line; we don't want all the extraneous details. We have the tendency to become overwhelmed by the expander's seemingly excessive use of words. I prefer communicating with other condensers, but when two condensers get together, their understanding may suffer from not enough openness or even a complete lack of communication.[42]

Expanders such as my wife prefer to spend several minutes elaborating with detailed, lengthy descriptions of all the thoughts, feelings, and emotions involved in every situation. She will definitely give the backstory behind every story. Expanders sometimes get frustrated by condensers who eliminate all the seemingly necessary details. My wife loves to participate in conversations with other expanders, but the problem is that two expanders might both be talking but not listening. Or after their delightfully lengthy discussion, they might look around and realize the event they were both attending has been over for some time.[43]

Expanders and condensers complement each other very well; many couples are composed of this mix and make a case for the cliché that opposites attract. This combo naturally balances each other's strengths and weaknesses but also presents a unique set of potential problems as each person is constantly receiving communications opposite to the way he or she is used to. It takes continual compromise and adjusting, but I've become a better communicator as a result. I now try to sprinkle extra details and feelings into my conversations.

The bottom line, spoken like a true condenser, is that everyone is different and has different levels of the amount of information he or she likes to give and receive. (I'll discuss this further in the "Personality Matrix" chapter.) There isn't a wrong or a right amount of information to give everyone you encounter. It's just good to know that the amount of information can create barriers to understanding.

Receiving Confusing Information Barriers—Say what you mean; mean what you say.

Sometimes, the actual information is the right quantity, but we send mixed messages that create confusion and make understanding difficult. We expect people to automatically know what information is valid and what isn't, what topic we've switched to, and which of the three or more conflicting emotions is accurate, forcing them to use their mind-reading skills to decode our messages and uncover our needs.

On July 8, 2008, I lost my dad to cancer. I spend time everyday thinking about him; I miss being able to talk to him. Shortly after his passing, my mom told me she had been diagnosed with breast cancer and had a large tumor. I was at work and struggling with completing my tasks and thinking about this new diagnosis. My boss, Rahi, happened to visit me later that day. He was probably the best direct supervisor I've ever had the pleasure of working for in all my jobs to date. When he came in, he could tell something was wrong. I wasn't my usual self. He asked me several times if everything was okay, but I just told him nothing was wrong in a somewhat bothered tone. I didn't want to let my emotions come to the surface for fear of a breakdown, so I repressed the news of my mother's condition. I just wanted to finish my shift.

My words were saying one thing but my actions and tone were saying something else. I was sending a mixed message of at least four feelings and emotions. Unfortunately, Rahi thought I was upset at him for some unknown reason and shortened his visit. After that, I noticed that when I would see him at meetings or during store visits, he seemed much more distant.

One day, he came to our store and went straight to the break room to eat lunch alone. I didn't even get a wave. That's when I realized the damage I had done with my mixed message. I went to the break room and explained the whole situation. My mixed message had not only prevented him from understanding my problem but had also led him and our relationship down the wrong path. I had created a strain with my all-time favorite supervisor.

Information Barriers

I have a tendency to reject information as I'm listening if it's in a negative form such as cursing or complaining or if it's illogical, ungrateful, argumentative, or fault finding. It's a wonder I take in any information at all. This is another style of communication that we learned as children; it's the old, "If you don't have something nice to say, don't say anything." When I hear things that are not nice, I tend to block them out or roll over them with a positive spin. For example, when my kids complain about anything, I'm quick to tell them how good they have it and go on with my life. When I would complain about not wanting to eat peas, my dad would tell me that kids were starving in China, and that was it. However, that did nothing for my understanding about world events or my father's understanding of my frustrations. And it didn't have a positive impact on our relationship.

Of course, I'm thankful my father was attempting to not let me grow up spoiled. Our children have the same complaints when we serve a food that may not be at the top of their lists. But we make an effort to show understanding before we encourage them to eat it. We might say, "I know peas aren't your favorite and you're upset we want you to eat them, but we have a responsibility as parents to serve you healthy food and teach you healthy eating habits." And I'll be honest—many times, we lose as parents and end up not making them eat it all. But almost every time this happens at the dinner table, we get some effort from the children. And we know they have a good understanding when we hear them repeat the encouraging talk to their siblings later.

When customers complain to me about service at the pharmacy, I have a natural tendency to reject it. When we tell customers that their prescriptions will be ready in fifteen minutes, some complain and threaten to take their business elsewhere. When my staff and I hear this complaint, we want to reject it because we feel fifteen minutes is a very quick time, and we know we're as fast as if not faster than our competitors. The complaint creates a barrier for us to understand their frustration; maybe they have someone waiting in the car, or a cab waiting outside, or a person in pain desperately waiting for the medicine. If we don't accept the information that they're in a hurry, we'll never understand why and therefore not be able to show them understanding.

I'm not encouraging that we just accept any information that comes our way or subject ourselves to a barrage of offensive language or personal threats. When that happens, I'll warn the person taking that attitude with me that I won't tolerate it. I've even had to call the police to remove such people from the pharmacy once or twice. But it's beneficial to receive negative information in the form of feedback, advice, or complaints; those who vent and complain the most have the greatest need for understanding. When I fail to receive the information, I miss a huge opportunity to show understanding and make a positive impact on the relationship. Some of the best relationships I have today began with customers complaining about something to me.

I have my share of customer complaints that haven't spawned the most beautiful relationships. My worst and most common receiving barrier to understanding comes when the information is tied to an "It's your fault!" theme. This is why many relationship books, especially those dealing with marriage, tell us not to use phrases such as "You always ..." or "You never ..." because such complaints are often taken as personal attacks. They cause me to go into a combative communication style, and I have a hard time not wanting to simply punch back with an accusation—usually ridiculous—of my own. When I do that, the results are never optimal, and very little understanding flows in either direction. I have to discipline myself not to take it personally.

When you get two combative personality types stuck in such mental and verbal conflict, even a tiny spark can create an inferno. Once, my direct supervisor (ex-military) sent me an e-mail asking if I had completed a report. When I told him I had forgotten to do it, the e-mail thread became worse and worse—texted punches were flying back and forth. I couldn't believe how an initial missed report could so quickly turn into me wanting to quit and I'm sure my supervisor wanting to fire me.

Fortunately, I realized where the thread was heading and asked the supervisor to call me so we could talk. He did so, twenty-four hours later. My request to talk and his delaying that for just a day was a great move on our parts; we both had time to simmer down and understand the other's situation. I learned that my boss was under immense pressure from his supervisor to have all the reports completed on time, and he learned this was a new report we weren't used to processing daily. But all the problems could have been avoided if I had just received the information that my lack of performance had created an issue for my supervisor.

Processing Barriers

☺☹☺

"I don't have time for this right now."

"At least you don't have cancer."

"Stop crying about it."

"Oh, I got it."

If I make it past person and information barriers, I have to think about the information. Among the biggest culprits that can block my thinking process are my emotions. That e-mail thread I just wrote about escalated in combativeness and became unproductive as emotions boiled over on both sides. We were unable to process any information until we allowed our anger to subside. Ironically, I need the most understanding when I'm the most emotional and attempting to explain something, but it's my emotions that can block understanding.

I see this when customers are upset and venting. Sometimes, customers will become very angry when we tell them we're unable to refill their prescriptions until we get a doctor's approval. Some become so angry that they can't process any information I tell them. Some have called our corporate 800 number to complain and then give the wrong information about the conversation. The transcription will show that they had trouble processing the names of the people they had talked to in the store correctly, basic details about their prescription, and what was actually said to them. Their emotions block their processing of the information and understanding of the situation.

Emotions are double-edged swords that can block our understanding as well as others' understanding. Angry customers will have a hard time processing what I'm telling them, and I'll have a hard time wanting to communicate at all. In fact, at times, we shut down the emotions coming our way. We tell people to cheer up or stop crying or quit feeling sorry for themselves instead of trying to understand their situations. I struggle when grown men are crying while attempting to tell me something. I know this is an area I need to work on, but I still freeze up and don't do a good job processing their information because I waste all my effort thinking about how to handle the situation.

Anger can be the worst barrier to mutual understanding. Feelings of anger prompt our innate fight-or-flight programming, and our adrenaline prepares us for battle or running away. It potentially creates combative listening and makes me do and say silly things I always end up regretting. I'm definitely living proof of this passage.

> Whoever is patient has great understanding, but
> one who is quick-tempered displays folly.
> —Proverbs 14:29

Even if I can remain calm, cool, and collected, I still have to put forth the effort to think about information to process it. That's why not putting in the effort to think is the common barrier to this step of the pathway. This probably seems obvious, but I see this barrier surface commonly in many not-so-obvious ways. For example, canned responses to others' frustrations don't require us to think. When we hear a problem, we tend to simply counter with a programmed response. I frequently ask my pharmacy interns what they're being taught about understanding. They tell me how they're told to say, "I understand you're frustrated about ..." and then fill in the concern. That's technically correct, but it can come off as insincere if the other person can tell it's just a programmed response. This tactic most commonly comes to light when a customer presents two concerns but gets the same canned response. A patient could say, "I have cancer," and a pharmacist might respond, "I understand you're concerned about having cancer." But if the customer then says, "Yes. It's preventing me from sleeping at night," and the pharmacist responds, "I understand you're concerned about sleeping," that's bad. Patients can spot parrots very easily.

The same thing happens when I call customer service departments and hear, "I understand it's frustrating when ..." I like to make up more concerns to see how many times in a row I can get the person to repeat that stock line. Pharmacy schools and customers service departments alike realize the importance of showing understanding to improve customer and patient relationships, but canned responses will never do that.

Another example of a nonthinking barrier to showing understanding is the old "It could always be worse" response. Yes, of course every situation could always be worse; people have a pretty good grasp on that one without its being pointed out. We all need to have a thankful attitude, but most people can have legitimate frustrations about situations that could and should get better. A dose of perspective can sometimes be helpful but many times it doesn't help to show understanding of the other's situation.

It's common to hear responses that start with, "Well, at least..." I sometimes hear people bypass someone else's frustration with a "Well, at least you don't have cancer." That comment can come from a good heart, but unless you're the patient's doctor, you don't know if that's true. Also, a doctor would unlikely use these words since many cancers are undetectable in the beginning stages. A response could be, "It's most likely that you have a low chance of being diagnosed with cancer in the near future," but such a response has no relevance on the person's current situation or frustrations, so why even go there? We can all be thankful for being cancer free and appreciate all our blessings. I encouraged this kind of personal attitude two chapters earlier, but the reason it's not helpful for showing understanding to others is because it doesn't require any thinking. You can reply with "At least you don't have cancer" to any statement of frustration. This approach is so common because it's quick, easy, and seems like a nice thing to say, but it's inappropriate.

Another convenient way to bypass our thinking process is to assume we already know the situation and thus not process any information we receive. We quickly say to ourselves, *I get it!* but many times we don't get it because we haven't confirmed or thought through the situation and tied the correct feelings and emotions to it.

> Any fool can know. The point is to understand.
> —Albert Einstein

I have looked foolish several times thinking I knew all about a situation only to find out I had no real understanding of it. I've been guilty on numerous occasions of thinking my wife was a hypochondriac when it came to our kids' health and criticizing her for hours of googling conditions and wanting to see doctors. After all, I'm the health care professional and should know if there's a real problem, right? Wrong! My wife's intuition has trumped me on almost every occasion. I've learned to understand that I have little medical diagnosing knowledge and need to leave all that to the medical doctors. When it comes to understanding the severity of any of our family's needs, nothing beats a mother's intuition.

People often complain when I tell them they'll have to wait more than thirty seconds for their prescriptions; they think all I have to do is slap a label on a bottle. What these upset customers lack is an understanding of everything involved in getting that label to print out. A prescription must be interpreted, input into the computer, and then checked by a pharmacist for accuracy, potential problems, and drug interactions. The information is then usually sent to an insurance company that determines the price. And there are usually at least ten prescriptions awaiting the same procedure that were in line before the upset customer dropped his or hers off. If customers understood everything involved, they'd be less likely to expect a correct label to just automatically print and be placed on a bottle containing the correct medicine.

Okay, sorry. My rant is over. But everyone has probably experienced feelings similar to this when others simplify his or her job or accomplishments because they thought they knew everything. Can you think of an example when this happened to you? If you can, try to remember that next time you're about to assume you know it all with someone else.

When we fail to think because we assume we already know, it's usually because we didn't confirm the facts with the other person. When we don't have enough of the facts, we often fail to give the other person the benefit of the doubt, and we fail to think about possible scenarios that could explain a situation. We fail to think about how we would feel if we were in the other person's shoes. While all this thinking takes time and effort, it can prevent a lot of communication barriers, misunderstandings, and conflict.

Thinking about the information that another person is attempting to convey takes the right state of mind. Fatigue, emotions, and attitude can easily stifle any chance for processing information and showing understanding. That's why timing can be very important. Picking the wrong moments can invite processing barriers to the party.

Showing Understanding Barriers

"That reminds me when I ..."
"Next time, just ..."
"This happened because ..."
"Why did you do that?"
"Same thing happened to me last week when ..."

The last set of barriers prevents us from *showing* understanding to others. Even if my understanding is right on target, it won't do much for improving a relationship if I fail to properly show it.

> No one cares about what you know
> until they know that you care.
> —Robert Cavett

Using an encouraging caring tone is a must. I've gotten into trouble on several occasions for expressing my understanding in a less-than-caring tone, using a robotic response, or speaking in a monotone. I have a natural monotone voice, while my lead technician, Sarah, has a natural, caring, and enthusiastic tone. When we both give an upset customer the same information and demonstrate we understand his or her frustration, many times, only Sarah's interaction with that patient makes a positive impact. I can use a lot of energy analyzing the problem, its cause, and a solution, so when I attempt to show understanding, I'm usually still thinking about everything else except my tendency to speak in a monotone. On the other hand, Sarah spends her energy attempting to make the customer feel better with her tone and attitude, and she naturally talks in an encouraging, caring tone. That makes all the difference regardless of the informational content.

My natural preference for my problem-solving tone creates another potential barrier to my showing understanding. I'm a natural find-it-and-fix-it type of person, but I've found that most people are looking for understanding, not solutions. On the occasions when they're looking for advice or a solution to a problem, that's usually made clear to me up front. My wife has told me on several occasions that I try to oversimplify situations with quick solutions or offer obvious solutions she could have come up with on her own. Whatever the case, the solutions do little for showing understanding.

One of my favorite movies, *White Men Can't Jump*, captures this point in a scene in which the lead character's girlfriend is reading a relationship book and tells the main character she's thirsty. The main character retrieves some water for her and considers the problem solved. The girlfriend tells him he's not supposed to get the water but rather tell her he understands what it's like to be thirsty. When I first saw this scene several years ago, I had no clue what it was all about; it just seemed like a typical trap men can never avoid, kind of like the "Do I look good in these jeans?" question. But today, after I have gained a much better grasp on understanding others, I totally get it.

The last barrier to understanding that I see frequently is when we show our understanding by telling a story of how we experienced a similar situation. While it can be good to let another person know you understand because you've shared the experience, a couple of problems can come up. First, no two situations are identical. I may think the same thing happened to me, but in reality, the circumstances can be and usually are different. Second, relating your own story shifts the focus from someone else to you; that can come off as you're wanting the other person to show understanding to you.

One hot Oklahoma night, I volunteered at our church to push buggies with crying children for three hours straight. After about ten minutes of that, I realized I had put on the wrong shoes. They were clamping around my feet like a boa constrictor and getting tighter with each step. Two hours later, I was hot, sweaty, and hobbling around, looking for water. Someone told me, "Good job on the buggy!" and said he knew how hard buggy duty could be. I immediately felt better and was happy someone understood my situation. But then he took off on a story about his buggy experiences. I began to feel he was trying to one-up me, and I thought he didn't understand my situation at all and was downgrading it with his comparison. As a result, his attempt to show understanding didn't resonate with me in a positive fashion. I doubt that was his intention, but that was how I felt.

I've seen the same reaction in others. Once, a group of us were at a family get-together and talking in the kitchen. One person told us how she was sore and tired from her experience at a fitness boot camp. Someone said, "Oh I know!" and explained all about her exercise experiences and the resulting fatigue and injuries. The initial boot camp person was upset and stepped out of the conversation. In both cases, people were attempting to show understanding but then described different situations and shifted the focus to themselves.

Pathway to Understanding

If you can make it past all the barriers to showing understanding, you'll have a chance to show it. But just as you can't automatically understand a foreign language, you can't just simply understand others. However, the approach to achieving understanding is similar to the approach to learning another language.

In school, to understand my Spanish lessons, I'd attend class, listen, take notes, ask questions, study, and think about the information. I was then able to show my understanding on quizzes and tests. This is the same recipe for relationships; the more work you put into your relationships, the better the results you'll achieve.

> The beginning of wisdom is this: Get wisdom.
> Though it costs all you have, get Understanding.
> —Proverbs 4:7

The first step to showing understanding starts with our hearts. We have to make a decision to remove all the prejudice and assumptions and caringly see others as individuals with unique situations who are trying to communicate their needs. We need to foster an openness that encourages others to share their information freely throughout interaction. We need to be present in the moment; we need to pay attention to others' content, tone, and body language. As information begins to flow, we must listen to and accept that information.

Next, we should identify and confirm the correct feelings and emotions tied to the situation. We then think about and process the information as we put ourselves in the other's shoes. We can then caringly and correctly demonstrate our understanding to the person. When others discover we truly care and understand their situations, that can be a powerful relational builder.

Be Present

Just as we have to attend classes to learn what we need to pass tests, we need to be present in relationships to understand. We might think we can simply get the notes from someone else and not go to class, but we would miss all the subtle verbal and nonverbal hints as to what might show up on the test. Those subtle notes make a big difference. I always did better showing my understanding on tests after having attended class. People would ask me how I was able to get certain questions right that they had gotten wrong. My response would usually be that I remembered the teacher saying it. So attend class in relationships by being aware and giving your full attention to them.

People will give you subtle, indirect cues. A talkative person suddenly becomes silent. Others say, "Oh great!" or "Why me?" When people post such comments on their social media sites, it's known as "vaguebooking." These are usually attempts to bait others into asking, "What's going on?" and an open invitation for anyone to show them understanding. As annoying as vaguebooking is to me, I realize it may lead to an important conversation. Some of these attempts are cries for help. I would hate to find out I was last person to hear a distress call before a tragic event. Even if these are minor situations, the fact that I show understanding can have major positive relational implications. So whether it's in the form of a status reply or face to face, make an effort to enter into an understanding conversation.

Many times, the cues are nonverbal—they take the form of body language. Knowing a couple of body language tips can help you understand when people are stressed or upset. I recommend any basic body language book, including *Let Me See Your Body Talk* by Jan Hargrove, to learn about just how much nonverbal communication we give off every day. We can easily deceive people with our words, but our bodies and tone usually always tell the truth. Just ask any world series of poker winner; it's very difficult if not impossible to keep our pupils from dilating when we have a great hand and are about to win a big pot. Knowing this can tell you when to fold 'em. Cue Kenny Rogers ...

For example, when you see another's arms suddenly crossing while you're talking to them, that usually means he or she is rejecting your information[44] and isn't interested in opening up but rather closing off to you. The time I went to the break room to clear up a misunderstanding with one of my all-time favorite supervisors, he crossed his arms when I walked in. That gave me a solid clue that he wasn't interested in receiving anything I might have had to say and that he was relationally guarded. But after I apologized and explained the whole situation, his arms uncrossed, and he asked how my family was doing.

Breathing deeply and then blowing out with your lips flapping is a stress indicator. Anytime I see and hear this, it usually means the person is under stress. That will prompt me to ask if everything is okay and hope I'm not the one causing the problem.

Finger pointing and hands on hips usually indicate frustration. Anytime I'm discussing an issue with my wife and

I see a hand go to her hip, I know I'm not doing well. If I see both hands on hips, that means I'm in big trouble. If I see the "human twizzler"—arms and legs crossed with her torso twisted to show me as much of her back as possible, I know I better get an understanding of the situation asap.

Being aware of these stress and frustration indicators can open the door to showing understanding while preventing conflict. They can help you smother a misunderstanding before it becomes a bigger problem and keep the human twizzler from becoming a human tornado.

Another nonverbal indicator is our tone. Our tone echoes the feelings of our heart. It's hard to hide stress and frustration with our tone, and it's hard to fake enthusiasm and caring with tone. A high-pitched response to a question may indicate deception.[45] When I hear everything is okay but in a mouse-like high pitch, I know that might not be the case. When I'm trying to show understanding in a caring tone, I have to think about how I care first and then let the tone naturally reflect my feelings; otherwise, my natural monotone tries to surface.

It's important to note here that though understanding tone and body language can provide good clues that can uncover feelings and situations, it's not an exact science—variations can exist between cultures, and different situations can appear the same on the surface. It's a good idea to confirm your discovery before making any assumptions based on any content, body language, and tone.

Recently, I had a stressful workday followed by a botched attempt at running errands, and that resulted in a long delay in getting home. I pulled in the driveway of our house and saw I had some missed messages from my wife. As I walked into the house, I noticed she didn't look happy. She was squinting as though the very sight of me pained her. I assumed she was upset that I was late and hadn't returned her messages. I was already stressed and thought, *How can she be upset at me after the crazy day I've just endured?* That assumption caused me to shut down and abandon my EQUIP model.

Shortly after making a fool of myself and storming off to the bedroom to make a statement of sorts, I learned she wasn't upset at all but was having a migraine. The purpose for her calls and messages was to let me know she needed Tylenol. I had completely misunderstood the situation. This is a prime example of the old assume line. (If you don't know it, google it.) Never assume. Had I simply asked what was wrong when I saw she was having a problem, I could have avoided looking like a male donkey.

Listening

After we identify a potential opportunity for someone to share information with us, we have to listen. To prevent listening barriers from throwing us off track and to optimize our effectiveness, use the following active listening techniques[46]; they will help you stay focused on the speaker while confirming the information you receive.

1) **Establish but don't overdo eye contact**. Like dancing, eye contact is an art that varies greatly in cultures and comfort levels. You don't want an intimidating staring contest or unknowingly offend someone. But having moments of eye contact during a conversation will help keep you focused and let others know you're paying attention. Maintaining an appropriate amount

of eye contact is a must. Keep your eyes away from a watch, clock, other people, or any electronic device.

2) **Make good use of head nods, eyebrow lifts, and other subtle but appropriate body language.** When we use these nonverbal expressions, they tell others we get what they're saying and encourage them to continue. But don't fall into the passive head-nods trap that doesn't match the dialog because you're suddenly daydreaming. Focus on the speakers' content and enhance your message back to them that you're understanding with these nonverbal encouragers.

3) **Elaborate nonverbal communication with verbal content.** Use phrases such as, "Go on" and "Tell me more about this." Sometimes, speakers worry they're talking too much and may not reveal some key information as a result. Encouraging them to elaborate can make them feel you care and therefore give you a deeper insight into their situation. I love to ask a lot of who, what, when, where, and why questions to encourage speakers to elaborate.

4) **Paraphrase the speaker's "bullet" points.** This technique keeps us from drifting off and forces us to focus on the speaker. It also helps us confirm that we understand what he or she is saying. If someone tells you, "Ugh! I got pulled over on the way to work, and there's no way I can afford it right now," you could say, "Oh no! You just got an expensive ticket?" to verify the content.

5) **Note verbal and nonverbal language alike.** Remember that most of what we say is not the actual content. Understanding the tone and body language can lead to understanding of the feeling and emotions of the message. You can confirm your notes with phrases such as "I bet that felt scary" or "That sounds frustrating" to verify your belief.

Active Speaking

The speaker can help the listener stay on track by utilizing some active speaking techniques. For example, the speaker can have the listener write things down, repeat phrases, and answer questions during the conversation to help the listener stay on track and not drift off. Our pastor, Craig Groeschel, is a master at active speaking. While he preaches, he utilizes all the above techniques and keeps us actively listening to his entire sermon, resulting in our deriving a better understanding of his message. If you want to see a great example of what active speaking looks like, I encourage you to visit www.lifechurch.tv and watch any of Craig's messages.

Receive the Information

Next, we have to keep the actual information from causing us to shut down the whole process. If we start judging, getting overemotional, defensive, and so on, it's difficult at best to show understanding. I really struggle in this area; I tend to take the information as a personal attack instead of keeping my perspective on the speaker's point of view. Simply put, we shouldn't take it personally. Even if it's a personal accusation, we can still receive it and learn from it; we don't have to let it make us angry. We can't control what people say, but we can control how we react to it. Easier said than done, but every time I'm able to overcome these barriers, the understanding I gain leads to greatly improved relationships.

I once faced a customer who accused all pharmacies of using expired drugs and demanded that we dispense medicine in the original bottle. I initially rejected the complaint because I knew our drugs were all a long way from expiring and I didn't like her angry tone. She would continue to come in and refill prescriptions while venting her frustrations to me and my staff. I'd dread seeing her come in because I knew someone would get an earful. It wasn't until I saw her as a person who had had a bad past experience that I was able to receive her information and move forward.

I told her I understood why she would be less than trusting based on what had happened. I explained we had strict procedures in place to prevent our selling drugs that had expired. I offered to pull any bottle off the shelf for her inspection. She was then open to my information about how we could reach a compromise with her request. Once we both received each other's information, our relationship dramatically improved.

When we know the truth, it's easy to reject false statements, but that does little to promote understanding. Even if the statement is false, it can explain why someone is experiencing a difficult situation. Sometimes, the statements are true, and we are the ones with the false understanding. If we receive information, we gain opportunities for improvement.

It's funny that we tend to not want to receive information because we don't want to admit the truth. We reject the information because in the words of Jack Nicholson, "You can't handle the truth!" We all want feedback as long as it's positive, but negative feedback in the form of constructive criticism, complaints, and frustrations can be just as helpful as positive feedback.

Every company has a survey these days for customers to rate their services, but I've found that many of those companies don't really want the surveys to give real feedback. This tells me they really don't want to understand their customers. Here's the problem. Many companies usually give surveys out while simultaneously begging for the highest marks; that's because many sales incentives and even jobs ride on the results. So giving honest feedback in an area in need of improvement could result in someone losing a job.

This is sometimes made clear to me as they hand me the survey. We give the highest marks, but the company has no idea how to understand any possible frustrations the customers may have, making the survey pointless. A better system would be to accept the criticism in the form of low scores and work on understanding why people have issues with these areas. Then show your understanding to the customer by improving in those areas. But as soon as you tie incentives and punishments into the mix, all bets are off. So leave those out.

Processing

After we receive information, we need to think about and process it; it's the processing that makes the lightbulb go off and leads to understanding.

> When asked, "Teacher, which is the greatest
> commandment in the Law?"
> Jesus replied: "'Love the Lord your God with
> all your heart and with all your soul and with
> all your mind.' This is the first and greatest
> commandment. And the second is like it: 'Love
> your neighbor as yourself.' All the Law and the
> Prophets hang on these two commandments."
> —Matthew 22: 36-40

Loving your neighbor as yourself, one of the greatest commandments, requires you to understand your neighbor's situation and think about how you would feel if you were in that situation. You have to process the information as if you were in the other's shoes. You have to treat others as you want to be treated.

I grew up as an only child and have always been used to my possessions being neat, tidy, and in like-new condition. I don't like to lend things to others because they rarely return in the same condition. Anytime a neighbor asks to borrow my lawn mower, I initially want to reject the request, but then I remember this commandment and I think about not having a mower but having a lawn that needed cutting. If I loved my neighbor as myself, I'd gladly lend my mower. That's what understanding is all about.

The only way to put yourself in another's shoes is by thinking about it. If you have a similar experience to call on, you'll remember what it felt like. If you don't have a similar situation, you can still try to imagine what it would be like.

Health care professional schools will sometimes have their students pretend to have a disease such as diabetes or asthma for a semester. The students will take placebos, monitor their conditions, and limit their activities to those of a person suffering from the disease. The goal is to give the student an understanding of what these people go through so they can better relate to them when they become their patients. They will have had an experience to think about. Of course, it would be mentally exhausting to attempt to do this for everyone in every situation; I'd never get any work done if I tried that. But picking the right situations at the right moments can have lifelong, positive effects on relationships. If someone is attempting to express a need or an emotion, those are good times to invest in understanding.

Sometimes, we think a situation is great because it looks good on paper. We can oversimplify a situation and fail to think it through. I thought it would be a good idea for my daughter, Meredith, to ride the bus to school since the bus stop was only two houses away. That way, she wouldn't have to walk very far, and my wife and I wouldn't have to worry about taking her to school in the morning. We went with that plan for some time. Then Meredith started to miss the bus in the morning because she was continually running behind schedule. My wife and I tried to get ready with her in the morning to fix the problem, but we noticed she was unusually quiet. We asked her if there was a problem; it turned out there was some bullying going on before the bus picked her up. I told her I'd go with her to get to the bottom of the problem.

I walked with Meredith to the bus stop and waited with her on the corner. Other kids started showing up one by one. I was interrogating them but wasn't getting anywhere. It was winter, and after about fifteen minutes of standing on the corner, I was freezing. I told Meredith, "Man! It's kinda cold out here," to which she replied "Dad, welcome to the bus stop." That's when it hit me. I never thought about anything else except the bus picking her up two houses away. I never processed her standing out in the cold for up to fifteen minutes while other kids were acting out. After that, I volunteered to start taking her to school.

Show Understanding

Now that we put in the time and energy to learn to avoid the barriers and understand the situation, it's time to properly show our understanding. The first step to showing others understanding is to remember it's all about them and their situations. It's easy to shift the focus to yourself, a solution, advice, or a lecture, but you should rather identify their feelings and caringly state them first.

The current buzzword out there to describe this process is "empathizing." Almost every leadership and management book has an empathy section. The definitions vary, but the common theme is one about putting yourself in the other's shoes, identifying the emotions and their causes, and caringly repeating them without sharing the feelings. When you learn that someone is frustrated about not getting many adult conversations in daily, you could say, "It must be frustrating when you go all day without adult conversation" or "It's probably hard and intellectually unstimulating to talk only to children all day long." In both examples, you repeat the emotion and cause to acknowledge the situation.

This method works great and keeps things on a professional level. When we don't share feelings or get emotional, that keeps things from getting personal. Also, not sharing feelings prevents us from getting frustrated, angry, or hysterical. That's what customer service departments do and what I do many times because it has proven, positive relational benefits.

My wife is very familiar with this method; she sees it coming from a mile away when I start a sentence with, "It's frustrating when ..." Even though she knows exactly what I'm doing, she still admits that hearing the empathy makes her feel better when she feels it's sincere. Just the fact that someone has put in the effort to understand her has value. If nothing else, it gives hope that her information has at least been heard by the other person. And if the other person is aware of the situation, there's a chance for assistance.

While we have to keep everything on a professional level at times, we can achieve a much greater relational impact by showing understanding while getting on an emotional level. A big problem with business and health care these days is that people in those professions don't make their interactions personal; everyone goes through the motions and fails to connect. Some think personal relationships in the workplace create bias and can even open them up to lawsuits. For example, just saying "I'm sorry" implies you were at fault. However, I believe the more personal things get, the better the results can be. When I was in pharmaceutical sales, personal relationships were everything, and I love the pharmacy customers I have personal relationships with. Those relationships make all the stress and hard times that come with the job worth it.

I like to expand the professional empathy model by trying to capture the emotions when I think about how I would feel if I were in the situation and then express that in my body language and tone. I may share the emotions especially if someone is rejoicing or mourning. And after restating the feeling and cause, I try to end with encouragement.

Rejoice with those who rejoice; mourn with those who mourn.
—Romans 12:15

I mentioned earlier how two people were able to connect with my wife and with me concerning my son's medical condition. James was the only person I can recall who wept with us. He shared the feelings, and his tears told the complete, heartfelt story of his understanding. Those tears were so powerful that I doubt I'll ever have a stronger relation with anyone else other than my wife concerning this issue. Many people reached out to us in a positive manner, and I am incredibly thankful for that. All the support helped us in our trial, but James's tears hitting the floor in our living room had the greatest impact on me.

Sharing joy can be just as beneficial and a lot more fun. If someone is experiencing a happy situation, becoming happy with him or her is a positive relationship builder. However, just stating robotically, "I understand you're happy" can be a buzz killer. What's worse is trying to wreck his or her joy Debbie Downer style.

One thing that prevents us from being happy when others are happy is perhaps the greatest focus shifter of all—jealously. When someone expresses excitement about going on a vacation, it's easy to feel jealous and start thinking about your situation rather than sharing in the joy. You might think you deserve a break more than the other person does, and you might start finding flaws with the other person's vacation to somehow make your situation seem better. I've seen this happen too often. It doesn't show understanding. When people are excited about something, expressing your happiness for them is a powerful relationship builder. "Wow! That's great! Going on a vacation is so exciting! You're going to have a blast!"

You can still reference yourself without making it *about* yourself. Sometimes, our trials and experiences are exactly what people need to know to help them get through theirs. Again, it's a matter of timing and intent. You don't want to prematurely inject your own story, so just wait for a green light. Don't do so until the middle or end of the conversation, and do so only if you feel the other person is open to your story. Whatever personal information you disclose must be wrapped in the intention of showing understanding to the other person—not shifting the focus to yourself.

Showing Understanding Step by Step

1) Open your heart to other people in their situation, good or bad, and make an effort to support them.

2) Avoid communication barriers to receive their information.

3) Use active listening to confirm key emotions and events.

4) Pause to think about how you would feel if you were in that situation.

5) Caringly state back the feelings and events without shifting the focus away from them.

Growing Spiritually through Understanding

- Proverbs 2:2–5: Turning your ear to wisdom and applying your heart to understanding—indeed, if you call out for insight and cry aloud for understanding, and if you look for it as for silver and search for it as for hidden treasure, then you will understand the fear of the LORD and find the knowledge of God.

- Matthew 7:1–5: Do not judge, or you too will be judged. For in the same way you judge others, you will be judged, and with the measure you use, it will be measured to you. Why do you look at the speck of sawdust in your brother's eye and pay no attention to the plank in your own eye? How can you say to your brother, "Let me take the speck out of your eye," when all the time there is a plank in your own eye? You hypocrite, first take the plank out of your own eye, and then you will see clearly to remove the speck from your brother's eye.

- Proverbs 18:13: To answer before listening—that is folly and shame.

- James 1:19: My dear brothers and sisters, take note of this: Everyone should be quick to listen, slow to speak and slow to become angry.

- Matthew 7:12: So in everything, do to others what you would have them do to you, for this sums up the Law and the Prophets.

- Galatians 6:2: Carry each other's burdens, and in this way you will fulfill the law of Christ.

chapter 4
invest

Do not be deceived; God cannot be mocked.
A man reaps what he sows.
—Galatians 6:7

You get out what you put in. You cannot expect to harvest any crops without preparing the soil, planting the seeds, supplying nutrients, and providing protection. You have to invest your resources to get a bountiful harvest.

This philosophy goes for everything in life. My alma mater, the University of Oklahoma, has a large statue of a man sowing seeds to symbolize this idea. Students invest their time going to class, studying, participating in activities, and paying tuition. The more they invest as students, the greater their educational experience will yield.

It makes sense that gardens, grades, or even retirement funds need continual investments to grow and flourish. But many times, we neglect to take this approach with our relationships. We usually put in a lot of time, effort, and other resources in the beginning, but then we go on autopilot and think everything will take care of itself—we stop investing in our relationships.

I can remember spending hours on the phone with my wife before we were married. Sometimes, we would spend thirty minutes making random noises. I'd put effort into finding out her favorite things and spend my money attaining them for her. For her twenty-first birthday, I rented a limo and took her out on the town. But ten years later, it seems I hardly have time to talk to her before we fall asleep at night, and all our money seems to disappear into the black hole of our children's needs. I know I need to continue to invest in her—I've written this book on that topic—but I catch myself slacking off at times.

One reason we slack off in our relationships is because our investment resources are finite. Whatever we "spend" on certain matters leaves us less to spend on all the others. This problem is the definition of opportunity costs. Spending the day golfing with friends will cost me the opportunity to spend the day with my family, working in the yard, and so on. If we spend $300 on groceries, we won't be spending that money on a night out. What commonly happens is that we invest many of our resources in the beginning of a relationship for entertainment and time together but then fail to keep investing when our resources are being spent elsewhere.

Another reason we tend to stop investing is because the costs of investing in relationships can be high in terms of time and effort. They can take everything we have at times to keep them going. Finding out your car needs some expensive repairs right during a rough week at work can be emotionally as well as financially draining, but when we shortchange our investments in our relationships, they inevitably decline. We need to continually pour ourselves into them to keep our relationships resonating like a well-tuned guitar.

The ideal scenario for relationships is when each side invests in one another; that creates synergy. When our resources are near depletion, it's nice having others investing their resources in us to keep things moving and vice versa. This allows us to accomplish more together than could be accomplished alone. In relationships, both sides can benefit from such mutual giving. Research shows that when we invest our resources by serving others, our blood pressure goes down, our level of happiness increases, and we add years to our lives.[47] All the benefits of good relationships with others is a current and future resource. Life is all about building strong relationships to help one another in our difficult challenges.

Two are better than one, because they
have a good return for their labor:
If either of them falls down, one can help the other up.

But pity anyone who falls and has no one to help them up
—Ecclesiastes 4:9–12

Because our resources are finite, picking the right soil to sow
our seeds in is vital. Just as we're careful about picking the right
retirement funds, we need to be careful with our relational choices.

Do not be misled: Bad company corrupts good character.
—1 Corinthians 15:33

We need to be wise about the relationships we invest
ourselves in. I'm not encouraging you to give up on people who
make bad choices, but if you invest a majority of your resources
in such relationships, it will be only a matter of time before you
start making poor choices as well. And we should not simply
surround ourselves with relationships that are flourishing and
neglect to reach out to those who desperately need us.

You'll know it's time to pull back from a relationship rather
than invest in it when the other person subjects you to continual
abuse, criticism, threats, or harm.[48] It's never a good strategy
to attempt to help someone if you'll end up worse off for your
efforts. Jumping into the ocean to save someone drowning if
you can't swim yourself won't end well for either party. You
need to know your limits.

We all have different levels of what we can handle. Some of
us can handle going to a bar to talk with a friend in a difficult
time while remaining an example of sobriety. Others, such as
myself, would be tempted to drink "just one more" and provide a
poor example. I'd be bringing myself down and failing to lift my
friend up. And the next day, I wouldn't be able to give my best
to any of my other relations; I'd be too busy nursing a hangover.

Keep in mind, however, the three special relationships we can never stop investing in. The first is God. I'll leave the specifics on this one up to you and your pastor. But even when things don't seem to be working out spiritually for us, we should never give up on God, who will never give up on us.

The next person to always stick it out with is yourself. It's sad when we let the pressures of the world bring us to the point that we let ourselves go. I've nearly given up on occasion and lived through some dark times without hope. I threw my health to the wind and lived on the edge. I understand how people can think the world or their lives would be better if they ceased to exist, but I know the power of Christ and what a blessing life can be. Take it from someone who grew up with yelling, mental abuse, physical abuse, abandonment, drugs, alcohol, dishes crashing, lies, letdowns, severe acne, late blooming, and personal addictions. You too can overcome your past and enjoy the blessing of today! I thank God every day for my beautiful wife and family and for the strength He has given me to never give up on myself. You too can replace your darkness with His light.

The last relationship to never stop investing in (except in cases of severe abuse or harm) is the one you have with your family, especially your spouse. You can't pick your family, but you can unconditionally love them. When you picked your spouse, you made one of the most serious commitments in your life: "Till death do us part." I don't mean to make you feel guilty if you're divorcing or divorced; I've been through a divorce, so I know all too well the pain and feelings of failure that come with signing those papers. However, I also know the positive benefits and generational impacts that come with keeping a marriage together. When your marriage is flourishing, the three key relationships are in balance; marriage is an eternal bond between the three people you need to keep investing in: you, your spouse, and God.

But remember the key to EQUIPing relationships is focusing on what *you* are doing. I recommend taking care of your own soil so you will be a positive light for others struggling to find their way. Before you start looking at others and deciding if it's time to invest or withdraw your resources, look at yourself—put your own oxygen mask on first, we're told. That's because it's much more difficult to help others when we're hypoxic.

Preparing Your Soil

I remember learning in business school about the Japanese philosophy called *kaizen*, "good change." Businesses use this model to continually improve their products or services by reducing inefficiencies. I immediately resonated with this philosophy when I read about it. I felt it was what I had been doing my whole life. I went to business school after completing my pharmacy degree just to improve my business knowledge. But unfortunately, I was neglecting my health, and that was having adverse effects on my relationships. It wasn't until many years later that I applied the kaizen philosophy to all areas of my life. I reversed my priorities; I put God first and started following the teachings of the Bible. Everything else fell into place, and my relationships underwent a change for the good.

Do you not know that your bodies are temples of the
Holy Spirit, who is in you, whom you have received
from God? You are not your own; you were bought at
a price. Therefore honor God with your bodies.
—1 Corinthians 6:19–20

If we want others to invest in us, we need to provide good soil for them to sow their seeds in. As we become healthier, so does the potential for our relationships since we are giving our best and being available. We need to invest our resources in things that will promote and maintain our own vital soil.

Sometimes, the first step is detoxing. If you are toxic and polluting your mind and body with unhealthy thoughts and habits, you'll find it difficult to lift others up. I recommend investing in the book *Soul Detox* by Craig Groeschel to help you identify and purify your toxic behaviors, emotions, and influences.

Next, we need to ensure our soil has plenty of nutrients. As a pharmacist, I know the importance that proper diet and exercise have for our bodies. Many of my pharmacy customers could stop taking their medicine if they focused in these two areas. Unfortunately, many of us want to neglect ourselves then cover it up with a prescription; too many of us inhale buttery, fried foods and take an expensive cholesterol medicine. Unhealthy diets create more problems than just the expenses and side effects of the medicine as well as bad lab values. The poor lifestyle choices and lack of nutrients can have adverse effects on our moods, concentration, and energy, and that can make it difficult for us to give our best to others.

Take two identical plants. Give one water and sunlight. Give the other soda pop and darkness. Watch the dramatic effects. One plant will be healthy and give off oxygen for us to breathe. The other will be wilting and near death; it will require significantly more resources just to stay alive. One will be able to give back to us. The other will take more from us.

When I studied leadership, I found that physical fitness is a commonly cited core component. Since leadership is all about relationships, that's not surprising to me. Physical fitness requires healthy eating, exercise, and discipline, but these investments yield many benefits.[49, 50, 51]

Eating healthy foods and exercising reduces our risk of disease and therefore gives our relationships more longevity as well as better quality. We can do more and for longer times. I became a father late in life, so I pray I'll be able to play with my grandchildren. My wife frequently reminds me of this desire when I make my food and exercise choices for the day.

Healthy lifestyles improve our mental health, and that makes us happier, more alert, and better able to concentrate; in addition, we become less subject to mood swings and stress. All these mental health benefits are positive relational builders. When negative mental health issues do surface, they usually require extra resources to get the relationships back on track. So avoiding a negative and gaining a positive is a double dose of good.

Physical fitness leads to weight loss, and that gives us more energy and confidence we can bring to our relationships. A healthy physique also gives leaders an extra advantage. Research shows that people are naturally drawn to and more apt to follow the lead of a physically fit person.[52 53]

Last, the discipline required to achieve physical fitness can spread to other areas of our relationships. When we train ourselves to put the donut down and eat a carrot, that habit can make it easier to turn down a sinful urge and focus on a positive relational builder. When I look to others for advice, I'm more receptive to those who show me they have healthy habits and discipline.

My wife is an ex-gymnast and has incredible will as a result. She's a living example of the Nike slogan, "Just do it" in spite of severe scoliosis, a shattered pelvis, and enough serious past medical battles to make every doctor who reads her chart whistle in amazement. She lets nothing sideline her; she runs marathons like Secretariat at the Kentucky Derby; she is fueled by the memories of doctors telling her she might never walk again. When onlookers see her running so hard, many say she can't possibly keep up her pace. But she never breaks stride; she knows only how to go all out.

Mary Ann also has an auto-immune disease that she often keeps at bay with diet only. Her specialist says her diet therapy is remarkable. It requires a lot of discipline for her to maintain her healthy food choices, so when my wife tells me anything about diet, exercise, or discipline, I listen! She's a great example of how to prepare our soil daily to maximize our effort.

We must carve out the time to get enough rest. This concept is so important that it's how the Bible starts. God spent six days creating everything and rested on the seventh. He commanded us to also work hard for six days and rest on the seventh. We all know how we act and feel when we have been burning the candle at both ends for too long; that's a good signal that we need to take care of our bodies by investing in rest.

While we're preparing our soil, we have to strive for a good balance between what we spend of our resources on ourselves and on others. We can and should treat ourselves well, but if our self-spending becomes excessive and our spending on others, particularly those with whom we are in important relationships, goes way down, we'll encounter relationship problems. The key is moderation.

The one thing that will always turn moderation into excess and cause one broken relationship after another is addiction. Drugs, alcohol, pornography, and gambling can have such serious impacts on resources and relationships, but even some not so obvious addictions can cause serious problems. They can cause people to lie, hide things, and disrupt their sleep cycles just as the major offenders can. They can also consume resources and leave little or none for relationships while transforming people into lesser versions of their true selves. I'm talking about addictions to social media, video games, work, exercising, and eating; these can all slowly take over people's lives and leave little room for others. And the little time left that can be spent with others usually includes the baggage of negative emotions—guilt, impatience, anger, frustration, boredom, and fatigue.

We all find ourselves getting out of control at times, but we all have a good internal monitoring system that tells us when that's happening. Nonetheless, we can always find ways to justify our addiction to that voice of reason; we can deceive ourselves all too easily. (Read *Leadership and Self-Deception* for more on this topic).

If we listen, our friends and family will usually tell us we may be putting too much time and energy into an activity and are risking letting it become an addiction. The more annoyed we become when others try to warn us, the more likely we may have a problem because we can very easily deceive ourselves, and before we know it, it's a full-blown addiction. That's the evil nemesis of positive relationships.

The CAGE test is a good tool to see if you may have an addiction or obsession with something that's depleting your resources.[54] If you have ever thought you should Cut back, or you get Annoyed when people ask you to cut back, or you ever felt Guilty about the activity, or it's the first thing you do or think about in the morning as your Eyes open, you may have a problem that is hindering your investments. If that's the case, please invest in some professional help.

> Those who work their land will have abundant food,
> but those who chase fantasies have no sense.
> —Proverbs 12:11

We are either working on important matters or spending our resources escaping responsibilities and idly sitting around watching TV, scrolling through social media, playing video games, and so on. I have a problem with the fantasy of video games, especially those on my phone. I often fail the CAGE test when I look at my game time. I know it makes no sense for me to play them when there are so many other productive things I could do with that time and energy. Every time I start to get out of hand, I get warnings from myself, friends, and family. My children will say, "Uh huh! Playing that game again." Some people will ask me jokingly if I'm addicted. Listening to others and my conscience is a good feedback monitoring system for me to know when to slow down. It makes a lot more sense to put the work into the relationships that can bear helpful fruit rather than into a video game; my smartphone game will never help me change a tire. Again, the key is moderation.

We all have some bad habits we know we need to work on. The good news is that we can take the resources we'd otherwise spend on our bad habits and apply them to our healthy habits. The Pulitzer Prize–winning author Charles Duhig explained how the key to exercising regularly, losing weight, being more productive, and achieving success is understanding how habits work.[55] Starting a new, healthy activity takes a bunch of effort in the beginning, but the more we stick with it, the easier it becomes, and then it turns into a habit requiring little of our resources because it—we—start working on autopilot. We spend our saved resources on developing new, healthful habits. This system can go on and on. The more I EQUIP my relationships, the more I can make positive impacts on people without even trying!

When I started running, I'd try for three miles but quit around the two-mile mark. I made quitting a habit. I'd deceive myself with all kinds of excuses—it's too cold, hot, windy, not enough wind, I ate too much, I didn't eat enough, God told me to stop—on and on. So my running coach, who is incidentally my lovely wife, helped me. She made me commit to finishing my next ten runs no matter the distance. It took a lot for me to finish them, but I did, and I developed the habit of finishing rather than quitting a run.

Nowadays, I waste no time or energy worrying about finishing a run. I don't have a ten-minute debate in my head during the run about finishing or quitting it. I use my extra mental energy to increase my distances and decrease my times. My runs have gotten longer and require less energy. And my newly developed habit of finishing spills over into other areas of my life. When I was writing this book, I kept at it instead of conjuring up reasons why I couldn't. That's the power of a positive habit.

After we've developed a good game plan for our health and habits, we can use some of our extra resources to invest in others and build positive relationships. To borrow a phrase from the amazing Christine Caine, we can invest our Time, Talent, Tongue, and Treasure. I have another T to add to the mix: Tenacity

Where we put our five Ts shows where our priorities lie and where our hearts are. There's no magic formula about which T will have the greatest effect, so I invest as many as I can.

Investing Time

Remember from chapter 2, "Quality Time," how to make the most of your time with others. Remember also that just being there doesn't necessarily have a huge impact on a relationship unless you're giving your full, focused attention. When investing time, make it quality time.

We can tell ourselves we don't have the money or energy to spend time with people, but we deceive ourselves this way. It doesn't require much to go to a park or the backyard and sit while the kids play or watch television with someone at a nursing home, or attend church with others while listening to the message. Even when I fall asleep on the couch trying to make it through a movie with my family, they know I'm at least attempting to invest my time with them.

One way our family donates our time is by going to our city rescue mission for homeless people. We attend a church service with them at the shelter and talk and listen to mission members while the children sing songs and play games with the mission children. It takes only four hours a month, but it has the potential to change others' lives forever by helping struggling people get back on their feet. This isn't to mention the benefits and changes our family receives by giving. All five of us look forward to the monthly visits and enjoy investing our time.

Most of us can say we live busy, hectic lives and don't have time for volunteering at shelters and such. Admittedly, I was reluctant to go the first and second times. And whenever my wife and I get invited over to someone's house for a get-together on the weekends, I often catch myself complaining that I don't want to spend my day off that way. My lovely wife reminds me that I need to put in the time to enhance my relationships. I know she's right, and I'm always glad I attended. I'm thankful to have someone in my life to motivate me to invest my time in relationships. The return on the investment is priceless.

Besides investing time *with* people, we need to also invest our time *in* people. We can take the time to memorize a birthday or anniversary and send a card or a message. We can take the time to mail a postcard or e-mail a photo when we're at interesting places. Anytime I know people were thinking about me when not in my presence, that always has a positive effect on our relationship.

The most important thing we can invest in when it comes to people is simply remembering their names; that can be a huge relational asset. I like it when people address me by name; that makes me feel memorable, and most people don't like to be forgotten. When I struggle to remember some of our pharmacy customer's names, I immediately get frustrated and angry responses such as, "I've been coming here for ten years and you don't even know my name!" I feel terrible when that happens. Remembering names is definitely a weakness of mine, so before I engage a customer, I ask other employees his or her name or ask the customer his or her date of birth and quickly check the computer for matches. After the customer leaves, I try to associate his or her name with a random fact about the person so I'll have a better chance to recall it in the future. I'll always remember the name of a friend's wife, Melissa, because when he introduced me to her, I thought of her as the singer Melissa Etheridge, and it's now stuck forever in my mind.

I feel that those who address me by name have made an effort to remember me and treat me as a person instead of a member of a collective group; that is a truly personal touch. When you address someone by his or her name, that's an immediate attention getter. Our names have been hardwired into our psyche since birth; we will recognize ours over any common word such as *hey* or *dude*. Continually repeating someone's name can also calm that person down if he or she is upset.[56] I do that at the pharmacy with irate customers, and it works.

Investing Talents

You can perform your talent for others and serve them for the short term, or you can teach your talent and serve them for the long haul. Make yourself a living example of the old Chinese proverb, "If you give a man a fish, you feed him for a day; if you teach a man to fish, you feed him for a lifetime."

We all have developed skills and abilities during our lives. You obviously have the ability to read, so you can invest in others by teaching them that skill. But besides everything we've been taught or learned on our own, we all have a special talent we were born with; God has given us all a gift, something special we can bring to the table. To borrow a line from Steve Harvey, it's not about doing what we're paid to do but doing what we were made to do.[57] We know when we're doing work that just doesn't fit us, and we know when we're engaged in work or an activity that comes naturally to us and requires little effort. Others often comment how good we are at it or ask how we're able to do it so effortlessly. Those activities are our gifts!

We have different gifts, according to the grace
given to each of us. If your gift is prophesying,
then prophesy in accordance with your faith; if it
is serving, then serve; if it is teaching, then teach;
if it is to encourage, then give encouragement;
if it is giving, then give generously; if it is to
lead, do it diligently; if it is to show mercy, do it
cheerfully.
—Romans 12: 6-8

In *Act Like a Success—Think Like a Success*, Steve Harvey
will assist you in discovering how to identify and use your gift
to achieve your goals. It's a tremendous blessing to discover
your special talent and use it to make a living and serve others.
I love and wholeheartedly agree with the following passage
from the book:

When we utilize our gift, the universe thanks
us by giving us an abundance of riches—from
abundant opportunities to good health to
financial wealth. When you aren't sowing into
the soil of the universe, you notice that things
in your life just seem to dry up and get worse.
But when you sow back into the universe with
your time, your passion, and your commitment
to others, the world will offer abundant
opportunities for you to blossom into the new
you. Incorporating your gift into your life and
sharing it with others will bring you joy, passion,
and a new vigor for living life to the fullest.[58]

Investing Tongue

I asked my wife what she thought my gift was. She told me I had a special ability to walk into a room of strangers and strike up meaningful conversations. I'm able to draw from my long list of experiences, good and bad, and relate to others. When I read the feedback I receive from students and sales reps after I teach them about pharmaceuticals, I am always shocked about how kind and powerful their comments are; I want to wallpaper my house with them. Any time I'm feeling down, I often pull up their feedback to encourage myself that I can make huge, positive impacts on people. For the rest of my life, I want to talk to people one on one and connect as I share what I have written in this book while learning from their experiences to continually network and improve.

This one-on-one talking has always been easy and natural for me. It's how I succeeded as a drug rep and what I enjoy most as a pharmacist. However, I've never been comfortable speaking to large groups. I understand the importance of such activities and have forced myself to get experience, hoping I would get better at it. But no matter how much experience I get, I'm never comfortable at a podium. I realize my gift is a soft spoken, private tongue that connects and resonates through written or one-on-one conversations.

I constantly use my skill by striking up conversations or keeping one going. I use it to prevent awkward silences from becoming uncomfortable situations. We've all been there— staring at someone on a date or a business function and having nothing to say. What happens? One party blurts out something so ridiculous that both parties cringe. I like to use these moments to encourage, build up, and learn from others.

One of my favorite opening lines is asking people what they're going to do on the upcoming weekend. Even when I've had a long day and don't feel like getting into another conversation, I still fire off this question. I love that many of my customers like to share their interests or professions with me. Not only have I learned a great deal about many hobbies and recreational activities, but I have also gained a huge reserve of professional friends I can consult for everything from lawn care to legal advice. And since the other person has the experience and expertise in their field, the advice I get can be a real blessing.

When I think of a more Braveheart-style tongue, I think of one that can inspire and motivate a large group to charge into battle with a "They may take our lives, but they will never take our freedom!" I think of my pastor, Craig Groeschel. I was raised by an atheist father and lived a life far from God. I never attended church much. I reluctantly accepted an invitation to attend Life Church with a one of my friends and his wife. The Life Church location happened to be where Craig was present versus a service that was taped or broadcast via satellite. I was instantly mesmerized and found myself hanging onto Craig's every word. He had a large and powerful presence that filled me with the Word of God. I felt he was talking to me personally. Through Craig's gift of teaching, I learned something about the Bible and immediately started applying it to my life. I thought church was cool and this pastor was a stud. I was in!

That was nearly ten years ago, and we've been attending and serving the church regularly since. My life, my family's lives, and possibly many future generations will be forever changed because of the gift of Craig's tongue.

Investing Treasure

Investing our treasure and giving to others is almost a sure bet on a positive relational return. The key word is *giving*, not *buying*. You can't buy love, but many people love it when you buy them things. Some people express their love through gifting, so as long as you're not attempting to manipulate someone or some situation through giving, go for it. And when others offer you gifts, don't deny their generosity and turn down such blessings. It doesn't take much to express your generosity and invest in your relationships. A drink, donut, or slice of pizza can boost a relationship with long resonating effects.

When I became president of the pharmacy fraternity, Phi Delta Chi, I discovered two things. One, very few members wanted to waste their lunch hours on fraternity meetings. Two, our fraternity had a pile of cash waiting for me to invest. I used some of it to buy pizza for those coming to our lunch meetings. I got some criticism for supposedly wasting funds, but attendance went from four or so to ten, then twenty, and then fifty and above. We started having productive meetings that generated ideas to bring in more money, and we increased memberships, and that meant increased dues. I was getting a true return on my investment of pizza. After two years of increased revenues, the critics went silent.

My first job out of college was as a drug rep. I remembered my pizza experience, so I invested in breakfasts, lunches, and dinners for doctors and staff at which I presented my product information. I learned that a $5 box of donuts could make an entire staff receptive to my presence. I faced stiff competition, but those donuts made the difference and gave me an advantage.

As a retail pharmacist, I experienced the other side of such exchanges. I had several sales reps attempting to push their companies' information on me. I also had had four or five bosses come in to give me our company's corporate information. I get bombarded with pharmacy patients who want to talk to me about everything under the sun. In all such cases, I have better relationships with those who come in with treats on occasion; that's a natural relational booster. You know they don't have to do it, but they do anyway. They spend their time, energy, and finances to bless us and tell us we're important and our time is valuable.

I work in a pharmacy building filled with aisles and aisles of drinks and snacks, so when things start to get stressful or one of my staff members does something great, I stop what I'm doing and get them a treat. I keep cases of bottled water in the pharmacy for anyone to enjoy at his or her convenience. The $1 investment can resonate for days and boost working relationships not to mention team and individual productivity.

Investing in family, friends, or working relationships is one thing; giving freely to strangers with no chance of an ROI, a return on investment, is something else. This type of giving goes against our natural self-preservation instincts and makes us true givers. If you had only enough money to eat for two days, why would you give away half and eat for only one? Because you have faith that God will provide not only for the second day but also many more. That's the "pay it forward" philosophy.

The Bible is filled with stories of how God provides for us and multiplies what little we have. The only challenge in the Bible God gives us is about money. He tells us to challenge him by tithing the first 10 percent of our earnings to the church and watch how the remaining 90 percent becomes greater than the original 100. Our church, Life Church, will even take the fear of losing the money out of the equation. It offers—to anyone, by the way—a three-month tithe challenge. At the end of three months, the church will give full refunds of tithes to those who don't feel God provided them any blessings.

Life Church is no stranger to unconditional, excessive giving of its treasure. It created and gives away free downloads of a Bible app called Youversion to those who want the Bible on their computers or smartphones. Over 10 million downloads have been made to date. Multiply that by ninety-nine cents or more and you realize just how generous this gift from Life Church has been. Life Church began with someone giving our pastor a free Bible, so our pastor gives out free Bibles. Now that's paying it forward.

> Those who give to the poor will lack nothing, but those who close their eyes to them receive many curses.
> —Proverbs 28:27

I have personal experiences with this proverb. I used to never give money to panhandlers on street corners. I thought they should just get jobs, and I was afraid my money would go for alcohol or drugs. I remember mocking someone for giving a couple of dollars each to the many panhandlers we encountered as we walked to a restaurant when we were attending a conference. I turned a blind eye. Then later that trip, the money in my wallet was stolen. I had over a couple hundred dollars of cash in it—the curse.

One year later, I planned to fly from Oklahoma to Florida to watch the Sooners play for the national championship. I wanted to surprise my girlfriend, now my wife, with tickets.

I'd already booked the hotel, flight, and rental car, but I was unable to locate any tickets to the game, not even overpriced ones. I was beginning to panic about the ticket situation when I saw someone on the corner with a sign asking for money. A big cold front was moving in, and I felt sad for the person, thinking he'd be cold that night as well as hungry. My heart told me to help. I rolled down the window and handed him the cash in my wallet. He said, "God bless you." My phone immediately rang. My hairdresser, of all people, told me she had a client trying to sell two tickets at face value. I lacked nothing.

Investing Tenacity

Finally, we need to invest in tenacity, the quality of firmly holding onto whatever we have set our sights on. It's when we demonstrate intense persistence, determination, perseverance, patience, endurance, tirelessness, and stamina to accomplish the goal.

So whatever terms from the above list you use to express your tenacity, investing it will usually create a positive relational impact. When I read through this list of synonyms, I immediately think of my wife. As a church volunteer, wife, stay-at-home mom, homeroom mom, friend, and athlete, she is all of these. She's special and uses her gift of tenacity to serve 24/7. I've never met anyone like her. She makes the Energizer Bunny look lazy. She's our tenacious Secretariat.

> The hardworking farmer should be the
> first to receive a share of the crops.
> —2 Timothy 2:6

Relationships require hard work. Anyone who claims relationships are easy and self-sustaining usually ends up with a list of failed relationships. I read an article once that instructed readers to move on to new relationships if their current relationships became difficult; that was an indication they were with the wrong person. Unfortunately, this philosophy is becoming the norm and is probably a major factor contributing to high divorce rates.

I see this same philosophy at work with many of my new pharmacy employees. Many want to quit after the first tough shift or even quit during the hiring and training process rather than putting in the effort to overcome their struggles. When we do invest the tenacity, the results can be positive.

When I see people giving all they have to whatever they're doing, they gain my respect and inspire me to work harder myself. One of my customers who happened to be running for a political office came into the pharmacy late one hot Oklahoma night. Her hair and clothes were dripping with sweat and her makeup was smeared. I asked her if everything was all right. She told me she had just finished going door to door in the area shaking hands and asking for votes. I remember thinking, *Wow! That's impressive!* She was putting in the effort, and it showed. It would have been easy for her to say that it was too hot or too late or that she wouldn't want to not look her best while asking for votes and then not put in the effort. But she did it. It was no surprise to me that she then became the governor of our state. I rarely voted up until that point, but her tenacity inspired me to support her. It wasn't her investments in campaign ads or the time she spent talking to me in the pharmacy about her aspirations; it was her intense effort knocking on doors that inspired me to help her.

When I was in pharmacy school and pledging to become a member of the Phi Delta Chi fraternity, I was given a blank book and instructed to get the signatures of all the current members. During our initiation ceremony, our books would be reviewed. I was scared what might happen to me if I didn't get enough signatures, so I became determined to get them all and started tracking them down one by one. I was one of the only pledges to take this challenge so seriously. I got about 99 percent of the signatures, and I even found some alumni to add to the list. Most of the other pledges were in the 30 percent range. The chapter president took note of my effort and asked me to think about becoming the next president. I eventually became the chapter president, which began my journey into leadership, relationships, and eventually this book—all because I invested in the effort to get those signatures. I still have the book of signatures that focused my life's direction; it was the first step in the journey.

We can improve our relationships in an infinite number of ways, but we still have to make the effort to tenaciously nurture them. We have to endure through good and bad times. The more effort we put in, the better the results.

It's not just what we choose to invest but how we choose to do it that is important. Investing in the name of fun has been a secret to my success. Putting resources into things that create smiles and laughter strengthens relationships fast and effectively. Fun elevates moods and increases productivity, and when others see you having fun, they want to join in.

Even a tiny investment can have a huge impact. I watched a social experiment—reality bomb if you will—in which a seven-year-old boy wearing a tattered shirt stood on a busy sidewalk in New York on a cold winter day. His sign said something like,

"Please help me. I'm homeless." The boy spent hours looking for help and even lay on the cold ground covered in a trash bag while hundreds of people walked by in their expensive suits and dresses. The people passing didn't even drop their spare change to the ground. Finally, a homeless man stopped to help. A man with little to nothing gave the boy the clothes off his body and what little money he had. Those little investments had an incredible impact.

The perception of the investment can also have a much greater impact as a result of the receiver's perspective. For example, give my five-year-old a bucket of quarters and he will think he's a millionaire able to buy every toy ever made. This is why children spell love, *t-i-m-e*. When I spent a day with my two-day-old son, that day is only a fraction of my life but half of his. While they are children, all the time I spend with them can still equal a majority of their lives.

Protecting Your Investments

After you sow the seeds, work the fields, and reap a bountiful crop, you need to protect your investment. The two most important relational protectors I've discovered are truth and humility. The armor of God is fastened with the belt of truth. The opposites of truth and humility—pride and lies—can quickly bring down even the strongest relationships.

> Three things cannot be hidden long: the
> sun, the moon, and the truth.
> —Buddha

Lying seems to be a natural defense mechanism we are preprogrammed with to avoid the unpleasant consequences of our actions or words. My toddlers were never taught how to lie but naturally did it when something mysteriously ended up broken. I had to teach them to tell the truth. I will watch them break a toy and ask them if they broke it. Even at ages one and two, they seem to instinctively lie and say no with guilty look on their faces or blame a sibling. As they get older and try to lie, their expressions and body language always gives them away. The older we get, the better we get at deception, but the truth always comes out. When it does, the results are a decline in the relationships involved.

When I catch someone in a lie, it angers me, and I play back all the lies in his or her tangled web that are revealed like dominoes falling. I feel foolish for having believed the lies and having trusted that person. The lies damage the relationship and make me less likely to invest more of myself in it. As a Christian, my job is to forgive and remember that I lie as well and to let God deal with it, but it's a real struggle.

> The wrath of God is being revealed from heaven
> against all the godlessness and wickedness of people,
> who suppress the truth by their wickedness.
> —Romans 1:18

Google a list of leadership qualities and you will find "being truthful" on nearly all of them. Truthfulness builds trust, and trust builds solid relationships. You wouldn't work long for a company that said it would pay you each week but never gave you a paycheck. The same goes for relationships with people.

We like to interact more with people we trust rather than with those we don't.

> Honesty is the first chapter in the book of wisdom.
> —Thomas Jefferson

Telling the truth is the smart thing to do; you will avoid the wrath of God and the wrath of those whom you would have otherwise lied to. Telling the truth requires much less effort since you don't have to waste time and effort inventing and rehearsing the false stories. When we're honest, we allow others the opportunity to help us.

One of the biggest lies I tell others is "I'm fine" when they ask how I'm doing. Many times, I'm not fine. I may be worrying about my finances, relationships, or health. One time, a regular pharmacy customer with whom I have a good relationship asked me how I was doing. I uncharacteristically complained about my back problems. The customer excitedly told me about a new product our pharmacy carried that could offer me some relief. I'd had no idea the product was out there. It immediately worked for me; I found some relief because I had been honest about my situation.

Many times, we're not honest and say everything is okay because we don't want to appear weak. We don't want to be complainers, so we put on façades; we give others a false impression of ourselves to look good in their eyes. We post the picture of the two seconds when the kids were smiling on a trip even though the other twenty-three hours and fifty-eight seconds of the day they were raging lunatics. We let our pride get in the way of the real story.

Pride goes before destruction, a haughty spirit before a fall.
—Proverbs 16:18

I've fallen on my back hard numerous times when I began to think I was amazing. God has a track record of humbling me at the pinnacle of my selfish pride. When I think I will dominate, I end up in last place. When I thought I would ace a test, I've failed. When I've thought I will impress someone, I've humiliated myself. Whenever I think I'm in control, God shows me he's the boss.

I once thought I could get myself out of a financial bind by working extra shifts. I didn't ask people for help, or pray, or invest. I signed up for several shifts and was making great progress until God stepped in and humbled me in the form of enormous vet bills. All the extra money I earned went straight to the vet. I've learned to put my pride aside and pray, increase my tithe, and ask for help. As a result, money comes in from all kinds of unexpected sources.

Pride can cause our strongest relationships to crumble. Every relationship will inevitably encounter a dispute or problem, and pride can keep us from moving forward as we do the opposite of the EQUIP variables. Our pride will lead us to believe that if there's a problem, we're not to blame. I love to blame ten people with no connection to my situation and then fault the United States or the world for problems rather than accepting personal responsibility.

I think that if it's not my fault, I have no reason to apologize. I forget that a simple "I'm sorry" can fix so many relational problems. And saying we're sorry or I'm sorry you feel that way are not apologies but focus shifters. Our pride won't let us admit fault, and that can damage our relationships for a long time. My wife and I have gone to bed at times both unwilling to apologize and playing the "If you touch my leg with your foot, I'll make you pay later" game. I've learned that it's better to apologize immediately to move things toward a healthy conversation.

Pride lurks and waits for the perfect opportunity to let a difference of opinion destroy a relationship by not allowing us to compromise. It keeps us from budging an inch or finding a middle ground; it tells us we're right.

> When pride comes, then comes disgrace,
> but with humility comes wisdom.
> —Proverbs 11:2

Leaders will take responsibility for all problems that happen on their watch and search for ways they could have personally prevented them. If your wife tries to back out of the garage before the door has completely opened, you could "blame game" her and do nothing for the situation or relationship. Conversely, you could say, "I'm sorry I put you in a situation in which you had to leave the house in a panic. I failed to plan correctly and created a hectic mess. I could have let you stay home and driven myself." Either way, the garage door is broken, but by humbly taking responsibility and not pointing fingers, the relationship won't suffer.

Our pride leads us to believe our bad situations aren't our fault, and pride keeps us from forgiving others. Humility tells us to apologize and forgive. A sincere apology can instantly repair a relationship and heal a wounded heart. Research shows that accepting an apology has a noticeable, positive physical effect on the body. Saying "I'm sorry" can instantly disarm an angry customer and allow a pathway to move forward. Saying

"Please forgive me" can powerfully strengthen a bond as an avenue of understanding and humble even the most arrogant.[59]

When a group succeeds, pride is the peacock that causes one of its members to say, "Look at me! It was all because of me" and try to steal the credit. The other members ask, "What about everything we did?" and the relationships decline. But when your team succeeds and you humbly give them the credit, the team's relationships flourish, creating a huge resonating potential.

When Kevin Durant won the NBA's MVP award in 2014, he gave one of the greatest ever emotional and heartfelt acceptance speeches. While trying to hold back his tears, he encouragingly and humbly thanked God, his teammates, his coaches, and his mother for helping him achieve the award as he explained the significant role each played in his journey.

Kevin started the speech by giving his appreciation to God not for winning the award or for his success but rather for the opportunity to be a platform to inspire others. Serving others is nothing new for this superstar. Kevin reminisced how his deep love for the game gave him the early dreams of using his abilities to help others as a recreational league coach.

He then confessed his early doubts about being a college athlete let alone the most valuable player in the NBA. To show his immense appreciation for the encouragement that helped propel him, he tearfully singled out his teammates, coaches, and organizational leaders by name and spoke about how they had affected his life. Kevin said that with those people behind him, he could do anything.

Kevin then singled out by name his friends and family. Tears of empathy fell from nearly all the millions of listeners, myself included, as he expressed his appreciation for all his mother's love and sacrifices—working hard as a single mother, making her children work hard, cheering from the sidelines, and going to bed hungry so her kids could eat. Kevin Durant emotionally told his mom that she was the real MVP. Finally, Kevin again thanked God for being the first and last and for saving his life.[60]

Kevin was honest and expressed his deep love for the encouragement and support he had received during the many hard times in his life. He didn't let the prestigious award diminish any of the investments he had tenaciously poured into his relationships throughout his career; instead, he wisely and unselfishly protected the fruits he had reaped with truth and humility.

Growing Spiritually through Investing

- Matthew 6:19–21: Do not store up for yourselves treasures on earth, where moths and vermin destroy, and where thieves break in and steal. But store up for yourselves treasures in heaven, where moths and vermin do not destroy, and where thieves do not break in and steal. For where your treasure is, there your heart will be also.

- 2 Corinthians 9:7: Each of you should give what you have decided in your heart to give, not reluctantly or under compulsion, for God loves a cheerful giver.

- Proverbs 3:9: Honor the LORD with your wealth, with the firstfruits of all your crops.

chapter 5
physical touch

Nothing is so healing as the human touch.
-Bobby Fischer

"Who touched me?" Jesus asked. When they all denied
it, Peter said, "Master, the people are crowding and
pressing against you." But Jesus said, "Someone touched
me; I know that power has gone out from me." Then
the woman, seeing that she could not go unnoticed,
came trembling and fell at his feet. In the presence of
all the people, she told why she had touched him and
how she had been instantly healed. Then he said to her,
"Daughter, your faith has healed you. Go in peace."
—Luke 8:45–48

This passage contains everything that makes physical touch
so important in our relationships. A woman demonstrated her
faith by fighting her way through a crowd and touching Jesus.
She had to be present and physically active, but that allowed
the transfer of a healing power. The touch fulfilled the woman's
need of healing and Jesus' desire for faithfulness. Worried she
may have crossed a boundary, she trembled and admitted her
action, but the result was a new, positive, personal relationship
between the woman and Jesus.

Physical Touch

The fastest way to create a positive, resonating impact on
a relationship is through the mother of all senses—physical
touch. Touch is the first language we learn in the womb and
usually the last sense to fade as we age. Physical touch is our
richest means of emotional expression and communicates a
wider range of feelings more quickly and accurately than other
forms of communication.[61] It literally connects us. That's why
when my children are scared, an embracing hug can calm them.

A tight grab on the arm can indicate danger and freeze them in their tracks in a busy parking lot. When my children are upset, I can tickle them and inject happy emotions into them, instantly transforming their mood.

Touch is so powerful that simply being touched by another person can trigger a cascade of chemical responses in our bodies that relieve stress and pain; create feelings of security, happiness, and comfort; enhance the immune system; decrease blood pressure; and improve blood sugar levels. Unlike the other EQUIP components, a lack of physical touch can lead to negative physiological and biological conditions including death.[62]

Newborns denied the physical touch of other humans can die from this lack of contact even if they have adequate food, clothing, and shelter. Infants who are touched gently on a regular basis gain weight and grow faster than babies without such physical contact. This discovery has led us to adopt the kangaroo care approach with our newborns; we incorporate adequate skin-to-skin contact starting at birth.

When our youngest son, Jacob, was born everything was going well until about 1 minute after I cut the umbilical cord. That's when he turned blue and stopped moving and breathing. The room became completely silent while we watched a nurse perform CPR on his lifeless body. My wife and I began to pray for a miracle —God answered. Jacob began to move and regain some color. However, the stress on his body was causing him to burn more calories than could be replenished by nursing. We had to let the doctor move our newborn to the neonatal intensive care unit for a two day feeding infusion. But before they took him away, the nurse made kangaroo time between

Jacob and mommy a priority. I remember thinking, *Wow this skin to skin thing must be really important.*

As we grow, if we don't get adequate physical touch, abnormal behavior results. Brain development in children is directly linked to the level of affection they receive. The lack of touch affection could have negative effects on their ability to later develop healthy relationships. They may have difficulty connecting with others, lack trust and self-worth, be afraid of initiating relationships, display anger, and be controlling.[63]

We need physical touch to thrive; our bodies are wired to receive it. Most of us have two eyes, two ears, a nose, and a tongue, but our skin contains numerous areas spread across our bodies that allow us to feel.

Research confirms the power that touching has on us. Patients report higher levels of satisfaction when their doctors touch them during exams. They can even feel that the total experience lasted twice as long as it did.[64] I can relate to these findings; my experiences with doctors are much better when they start things off with a handshake.

A recent study looked at the touch rates of professional basketball players. When they counted the number of times pro basketball players touched each other during a game, they found that the teams with a lot of physical touch were in the top of the league and the teams with the lowest touching were at the bottom.[65]

I experienced this sports teammate touching correlation when I played in a pickup basketball game between pharmacy school classes. One time, a group of medical school students needed one more player, so they let me, a pharmacy student, play on their team. I just knew I wouldn't get a lot of passes and would have to work hard to get the ball and have a chance to score. These medical school guys were extremely competitive; they made it clear to me that I had better not blow it for them.

The game was tied 15–15 when suddenly I got a pass and had an open three-point shot. I took the shot. I made it! I thought, *Thank you, Lord, for helping that one go in. Okay, cool. I'll just play good defense and get through this game without any problems.* Unexpectedly, one of my teammates gave me a side-five slap on my hand and said, "Nice one, guy. That was huge." That physical touch sparked a scoring frenzy in me that helped us win that game and several more that day. The physical touch transformed me; it boosted my confidence, ability, and productivity. It wasn't the encouraging words or the fact that I had made the shot; it was the power I felt after that hand slap. It was one of those strange and magical sensations I'll never forget.

Physically touching people is a huge relational builder, but there is an important prerequisite to it all. We also have to be physically present in order to touch anyone. At times, we have to get out of our thinking and into our doing. We have to get off the sidelines and into the game. We have to break a sweat and get our hands dirty to make something happen. Our actions speak louder than our words.

Well done is better than well said.
—Benjamin Franklin

Take a football team for example. Coaches analyze the defense and direct the players. Excited cheerleaders encourage the team. Referees keep the peace. Still, someone has to physically touch the football and get it into the end zone. The same goes for our relationships. Sometimes, to move things forward, we have to get our hands involved and take action.

We can't do that if we're not present. That fact is becoming ever so important for the increasing number of people who work from home and communicate via phone and e-mail. They can't physically touch others. They can forget how to interact with touch or not even learn how to touch in the first place due to their isolation. The woman seeking Jesus didn't stay home and pray for healing, or ask one of her friends to tell Jesus to heal her, or send Jesus a friend request; she sought him out and touched him.

We all have excuses for not going to see a person or event. I use some all the time. We say, "I need to relax," "Maybe next time," "I made other plans," and so on. Then we stay home and miss an opportunity to be physically present and do something with our hands for ourselves or for someone else.

Even when I do make it out, I can catch myself on the sidelines thinking but not doing. One time at a swim party, a child was discovered lying on the bottom of the pool. Chaos ensued. A large crowd gathered. I tried to analyze the situation but completely misinterpreted it. I thought I had heard and saw two children jump into the pool at the same time and bump heads. I had no idea that a child was in desperate need of CPR. What's worse was that I was the most qualified person present to administer CPR. I needed to physically touch the child while making my assessment and be more active with my questions rather than assuming I understood the situation. Thankfully, through God's will, the child made a full recovery. But to this day, my lack of action haunts me. I was present but had no physical presence.

However, a brave ten-year-old, my daughter, Meredith, had a physical presence. Amid all the panic, Meredith jumped into the pool and dragged the drowning child out of the water. In situations like that, every second counts. I couldn't have been any prouder of Meredith. The city of Edmond shared my feelings; the mayor presented her with a medal and certificate at a Proclamation of Honor Ceremony. Had the person who had discovered the child or Meredith not been present and physically acting, this story could have had a tragic ending. Never underestimate the power of being physically present and ready to act. You never know how God might use you.

Many times, we are present but fail to physically get our hands on anything because we talk ourselves out of acting. The woman who touched Jesus could have seen the large crowd and noticed Jesus was in a hurry to get somewhere and told herself, *Maybe next time* or *Sheesh, the crowd is too big for me to get to Him*. She could have second-guessed it away with a *Maybe I don't deserve to be healed*. Instead, she took action and fought her way through the crowd to physically touch Jesus.

Once, I saw my wife watering her garden. I went out to talk to her and see how the harvest was coming. It was a hot, sunny, Oklahoma summer day, but I wanted to be physically present in my wife's life. My wife noticed some weeds that needed pulling, so she started in on them. I figured it would take her well over thirty minutes to get them up. I knew that if I jumped in, I'd end up a sweaty mess and would need a shower. But I couldn't be present and not physically act. I plopped down and pulled weeds shoulder to shoulder with her as sweat dripped down my nose. I felt compelled to get my hands dirty. I know she appreciated the help, and it boosted our relationship. On top of that, I enjoyed helping and accomplishing the goal together just as much if not more. It was definitely a win-win.

The only losers that day were the weeds; they may have not liked the way I touched them, but they weren't likely to call the police and slap me with a sexual harassment lawsuit. However, *people* can and often do when they feel they've been touched inappropriately. Before we get into the physical touching of people, we need to address a little thing called boundaries.

We all have different levels of what we are comfortable with when it comes to others' touches; these are our boundaries. Some people become uncomfortable when another person gets too close to their personal space. One person's boundary may be absolutely no touching at all while another person may be comfortable with a hug as he or she is introduced for the first time, but any touching that violates his or her personal limit could result in anything from discomfort, anxiety, and anger to assault and even a lawsuit.

No two people are alike when it comes to these invisible barriers. Their experiences, religion, ethnicity, childhood teaching, and culture can all have an effect on their touching preferences and boundaries.

My two sons have very different physical touch preferences. Mason is the cuddler while Jacob is the warrior who loves to initiate touch with playful punching, kicking, dog piling, and wrestling. He would much rather fly off the bed like Superman and knock me to the ground than hug me. Jacob is only three but is already physically superior and more coordinated than his father! He loves to tirelessly demonstrate his dominance as an avenue to fulfill his physical touch needs.

You might think that slapping others on their heads or pouncing on colleagues and knocking them down are inappropriate forms of physical touch, but you'll readily see such behavior between teammates in football games. They use such forms of physical touch to show appreciation and enthusiasm for their teammates. That's the culture for athletes, but it's definitely not appropriate in most other situations. I'd never engage in such shows of affection or appreciation at the pharmacy if only because it's not my natural preference.

I was an only child who grew up with little physical touching at home. I can count on my hands the number of times I was hugged by my dad, and I can't remember witnessing any physical touch between my parents. Our relationships suffered as a result and prompted some abnormal behavior on my part.

As I grew up, I rarely touched others; I appeared cold and insensitive on many occasions. Whenever someone would unexpectedly slap me on the back to express congratulations, I would jump, shake, and nearly fall to the ground. Even today, I sometimes jump when my wife unexpectedly rubs my back in the morning. But having learned the importance of touch, I've learned to make the effort to touch others. I consciously use my EQUIP model to incorporate physical touch into my relationships and take action.

And I'm not alone. Studies show that Americans are significantly less likely to touch one another when compared to people from other countries. Interestingly, people in Paris, the Mediterranean, and Puerto Rico touch one another the most.[66] I'm not surprised Americans end up low on the touching list; it seems they are borderline touch-a-phobic. Alcohol hand sanitizer flies off the shelves at our pharmacy, and customers complain if I don't have some available at the register for them to use after touching something that other customers had recently placed their hands on. The silver lining is that with this reluctance to engage in physical contact, knowing how to use touch can be your secret weapon for relationships.

Imagine the dirtiest and smelliest feet you have ever come across. (Hopefully they aren't yours.) Can you picture them? Maybe even a little bit slimy with some thick calluses and perhaps a scab or two. If those feet belonged to one of your employees, would you volunteer to hand wash them before they started a shift? That's exactly what Jesus did for his disciples. And if you think hygiene is bad these days, just imagine what it must have been like over 2,000 years ago.

> Now that I, your Lord and Teacher, have washed your
> feet, you also should wash one another's feet.
> —John 13:14

My close friend Sarah often tells the story of when one of Oklahoma's former governors came into the pharmacy eating an ice cream cone. Her eyes lit up as she excitedly admired the delicious treat. As soon as the governor noticed Sarah's interest, he held out the ice cream cone and offered her a lick. Sarah was stunned; she couldn't believe he would trust her to touch the ice cream with her tongue and give it back. That gesture took the relationship to a completely new level and bonded her to him ever since. The governor knew the secret resonating weapon of touch.

So how do we know when we can make the effort to physically touch others without crossing their boundaries? There's no way to know. Any time we put our hands on someone, there's always a potential for things to go wrong. But touch is too important in relationships to fear the worst and simply refrain from touching. Consider the following physical touch barriers before engaging in the act.[67, 68, 69, 70, 71]

Hygiene Boundary

If your hands are dirty, sweaty, or wet, be courteous—don't put them on anyone until you've taken care of the issue. At the same time, don't let someone else's poor hygiene prevent you from making contact. If someone shakes your hand and leaves an unknown gift, simply wash your hands before you eat. You'll most likely survive and end up with a better relationship. But don't clean your hands immediately following the handshake in the presence of the other person. A corporate visitor came to our pharmacy, and I shook his hand. He immediately dove for some hand sanitizer and vigorously started cleaning his hands. I felt embarrassed; it was as if I'd had a contagious disease.

Off-Limits Boundary

There are body parts you should never touch; touching others' private parts or even your own is an absolute no-no. Even if you do it as a joke or as an example of what someone else had done to you, you could end up in big trouble. Check with your HR department's policy for a complete list of forbidden touching. I've learned that if I cross my wife's touching boundaries, many things will suffer, usually as a result of a karate move.

Permission Boundary

When you touch others, pay attention to their body language. If they lean away, frown, or run, that means they're uncomfortable. And no means no. If others even jokingly mention they're uncomfortable with your touching them, take them seriously. If someone asks you point blank to stop, do so without hesitation and apologize.

Emotion Boundary

Never touch out of negative emotions such as anger or frustration. Bully touching such as poking your finger into others' chests or grabbing their arms to jerk them aside can get you in big trouble and have a negative impact on a relationship. However, a loving or caressing touch at work can be just as detrimental. Your touch conveys your emotions, so save the love touches for the appropriate personal relationships. If you become romantically aroused or express inappropriate interest in someone by touching him or her, those emotions are going to come through and you will come off as a creep.

Be extremely cautious if you touch an upset person because that might prompt a retaliation touch such as a push, shove, or punch.

Precedence Boundary: Monkey See, Monkey Do

Some people are uncomfortable with physical touch because they don't want to set a precedent that's it's okay for anyone to touch them in a similar manner. For example, some people in a large crowd may turn down a handshake if they're not ready to shake everyone's hand. If a boss allows a subordinate to embrace or hug him or her, other employees might try the same thing. I know by experience, and emails from the principal, that kids will do everything they see their parents do.

Relationship Boundary

Know the relationship and pick the appropriate touch. Pats on the back or light arm punches can be too much for some people until you know them better. With someone you have just met, start off with a handshake. When your arm is extended, you're asking the other person for permission to make contact; the other person has the option of denying or modifying it.

After you're confident you won't encroach on boundaries, you can make the effort to appropriately physically touch someone based on the relationship. Let's break physical touch down into professional and personal touching and then sexual and nonsexual touching (NST). Professional touch is for your business relationships, nonsexual for your family, and sexual for your spouse. Friends fall between professional and nonsexual depending on how strong the friendship is and any boundary issues.

Professional Physical Touch

We can engage in all kinds of appropriate professional physical touching at work, but rather than assuming we know them all, we should check with our HR departments first. Most HR cases stem from quid pro quo rubbing, stroking, remaining in someone's personal space too long, or using too much force. When we touch someone, we're displaying our emotions, so touching out of lust or anger will almost always result in an issue. For professional relationships, I keep contact in the shoulder to the hand zone with occasional upper back. The positive emotions I convey are excitement, appreciation, and understanding with an encouraging mind-set.

A mentor of mine in pharmacy school was a high fiver. He was constantly walking the school halls dishing out high fives to students. As a result, many of us felt he had a better relationship with us than did any of the other faculty. We felt he cared about us and wanted a deeper relationship than just teacher and student. It would have been impossible for him to have conversations with multiple students as we all scurried to get to class, but every time we saw him in the halls and he slapped our hands, it strengthened our relationship. He was able to get much more out of his presence.

At our graduation, after he finished talking to the hundreds of us in the audience, he left the podium and walked past several rows of students. I couldn't pass up the opportunity for one last high five from him. I held my hand high. He slapped it so hard that it rocked the entire auditorium. I couldn't have asked for a better ending to my graduation or beginning to my career. I knew I was going to carry his physical touch torch into my professional relationships.

It has served me well. Studies confirm that physical touching in the workplace increases productivity. People who give and receive more physical contact are more likely to volunteer for extra assignments[72]. I use the following forms of professional physical touch with my employees, bosses, customers, new acquaintances, and so on: handshakes, high fives, fist bumps, back pats, back drums (two-handed back pat), arm knocks, and side hugs to connect and attempt to show them appreciation and encouragement.

The Handshake

There are many ways to shake someone's hand, but every time I try to do the new, "cool" handshake, I mess it up and look ridiculous. I never fare well when I'm trying to be someone I'm not. I found it best for me to stick to the traditional hand extended straight out with palm neither up nor down, firmly grasp the other's hand, and give a single shake. That's the technique my father taught me when I was ten. I'm confident with this shake, and it translates with my action.

You'll find many articles and books on handshaking. A lot of judgments and insights can be made immediately after shaking a hand. Some people use handshakes to establish dominance, but if you want to build relationships, just shake someone's hand to express your positive feelings. When your heart is in the right place and you extend your hand, that feeling will be translated.

Many folks fear handshakes because of germs. We pick up germs in all kinds of places, not just from hands. The key is good hygiene. Simply don't touch your mouth, eyes, or nose until you wash your hands, and wash your hands before you eat. Follow good hygiene and feel free to touch people. What surprises me is that many health care providers understand this good hygiene concept but fail to shake hands.

When I go to a clinic to have a physician check me out for a sore throat or fever, I notice that younger doctors are much less likely to shake my hand when they walk into the room. Older doctors, however, start with their arm extended. I have better experiences with the handshakers; I feel they care more about me and my condition.

That initial handshake or other form of physical touch can set the stage for the rest of the interaction; it can make or break a relationship. I like to use handshakes for initial introductions to show others I'm glad to meet them, to close a deal and show others they can trust I'll fulfill my end of the agreement, as the default physical touch option for relationships that are still on the surface, and as a sincere thank you.

The High Five

The high five is the hand held high with the palm facing the other person with the expectation he or she will slap your hand with an open palm. Sometimes, we have to coax others to slap our hands with a "You're leaving me hanging." No one likes to be left hanging. I use the high five to connect with others and share excitement and enthusiasm.

Fist Bump

When you hold your arm out in front of your body with your hand in a fist, you're expecting the other person to do the same and lightly bump your fist. You can then blow it up by making an explosion sound while fully extending your fingers. My greatest fist bump to date was recently with Charles Barkley.

I use the fist bump as an alternate to the handshake when either my hands or the other person's hands are dirty or wet. I don't want to have to explain why my hands are wet or dirty but still want to connect.

Back Pats

Who doesn't like pats on the back? It's the traditional way to express approval for a job well done. When we boast about our accomplishments, someone will usually say, "Don't break your arm patting yourself on the back." That's exactly what I use it for—not for myself but for others. I frequently walk by my employees and pat them on their backs as I say, "Good job!" I also use it to encourage people in stressful situations and say, "We'll make it through this."

Back Drums

This is a light, two-handed back pat I use when I want to express my appreciation for a job well done. It's about five beats long and expresses my enthusiasm. I also use back drums for stressful moments to break the tension. I'll use back drums in professional relationships that are already strong, but if I back drummed a new acquaintance, he or she might call 911.

Arm Punch

This is a light, closed-fist tap on a person's upper arm. I use it when I want the other person to feel strong about an accomplishment. I also use it to break tension or get someone's attention; I'll leave my fist pressed against his or her arm until I get a response. It usually gets the recipient to smile and shift focus to me.

Rear-Out Hug

This hug variation is gaining popularity and becoming a frequent addition to an introductory handshake. It's a face-to-face hug with the torsos bent 45 degrees to create a significant distance between the waists of the huggers. Both people push their rear ends away from each other to demonstrate the hug has no affectional intentions.

Side Hug

The side hug is when I hug someone's shoulder from the side rather than from the front. This style keeps me from getting into their personal space and is a less-personal style of a hug. I use the hug to show a deeper appreciation than what I'd show with a handshake. I've found the older female customers really enjoy this one, but I'd be hesitant to side hug a younger female—my age or younger—since I wouldn't want to give the impression of a personal touch.

I remember one time as a drug rep showing up to work with a doctor for a day as an educational experience. I thought it was going to be a good day and wonderful learning experience for me as well as a great opportunity for me to build rapport with a difficult-to-see doctor. But right as I walked in, this guy started bashing me on everything from my wardrobe to my career choice. After enduring fifteen minutes of constant ridicule, I lashed out with an offensive comment and prepared to leave. Instead of letting me leave, the doctor gave me a big side hug and apologized. I distinctly remember feeling his remorse and concern. That hug made me feel things that no words could have accomplished and was the beginning of a great professional relationship.

Personal Physical Touch: Nonsexual (NST)

Physical touch in our personal relationships is perhaps the most powerful way to create chemistry and intimacy and thus strengthen bonds.[73] In our personal relationships, the stakes are higher. They become a prerequisite for every healthy relationship and create a fundamental avenue for giving and receiving affection. Besides promoting all the previously mentioned biological benefits such as decreased stress and improved mood, personal touch can make us feel accepted and loved, and feeling loved by another might just be the most important feeling a human can experience.

Physical touch is considered by many to be a love language. Gary Chapman wrote this about physical touch in his book *The 5 Love Languages*.

> Almost instinctively in a time of crisis, we hug one another. Why? Because physical touch is a powerful communicator of love. In a time of crisis, more than anything, we need to feel loved. We cannot always change events, but we can survive if we feel loved.[74]

When those you have personal relationships with experience inevitable crises in the forms of serious automobile accidents, difficult medical diagnoses, deaths of family members, or other such tragedies, the most important thing you can do for them is make them feel loved.

Anytime my wife tells one of her friends about a very difficult situation in her life and the listener responds with a hug, that brings tears to her eyes. There's something about that form of physical touch that taps deep into her soul. She becomes overwhelmed with all the emotions involved, and she processes them instead of suppressing them. And her relational bonds with the huggers are greatly improved.

Professional physical touch can be dialed a notch up to personal physical touch. Personal touch will increase affection and arouse feelings of love in the giver and recipient. (This is not to be confused with feelings of lovemaking, which I'll handle in the sexual touch section.) This type of touch is for family and personal friends such as girlfriends, boyfriends, and so on. It's the type of touch that lets others know they have our hearts, and it reinforces intimacy.

The following list comes from studies centered on affectionate touching. And most examples of other types of personal physical touching (NST) can usually be reduced to fit one of these categories.[75, 76]

- holding hands
- full hugging
- cuddling/holding
- caressing/stroking
- kissing on the face
- kissing on the lips
- backrubs/massages

These are the keys to healthy personal relationships that protect against the inevitable storms and help resolve conflicts. They express understanding, value, and security. I never miss an opportunity to hug and kiss my children. You can never give your kids too many "I love yous" in the form of hugs and kisses. I can't even walk by them without rubbing their heads or backs; showing them such affection is just my natural and almost involuntary response.

Unfortunately, I struggle with doing the same with my wife. I love her equally but fail to express it to her through NST. My thoughts are there, but my actions don't express them. I often think about how much I love her, but I fail to express it. This is an issue with many married couples. It's too easy to focus on the children and neglect the one who gave them to you. It's too easy to get caught up with life and let that initial fire that consumed you initially start to burn out. Using the EQUIP approach has reminded me on several occasions to incorporate the physical touch she craves.

When I was working on this chapter, I stepped things up, and she loved that. I know how important it is to her, so I try my best to come up with new ways to make her feel loved through my touch. I like to give her bear hugs when I walk by her in the house, hold her hand, or walk shoulder to shoulder when we're out. I recently stumbled upon a new tip of opening her car door and caressing or stroking her as she gets in.

One of the biggest problems I have with giving my wife NST is that she's the sexiest woman alive; I naturally want to default to sexual touch with her. But as most women will tell you, it's the NST that leads to the ST.

Let's talk about the special and magical physical touch that is reserved for spouses—sexual touch. This type of touch stimulates our erogenous zones and leads to fruitfulness and multiplication. A whole section of the Bible is devoted to God's words about the joy and pleasures sexual touch can bring a husband and wife. It's found in not just a verse or two but in the many chapters of the Song of Solomon. While some of the information may seem cryptic, when read from a lover's point of view, it sends a clear message. Here are a couple of verses just to give you an idea.

> [Solomon to his wife:] Your stature is like
> that of the palm, and your breasts
> like clusters of fruit. I said, "I will climb the
> palm tree; I will take hold of its fruit."
> —Song of Solomon 7: 7-8

> [Wife to Solomon:] Awake, north wind, and come,
> south wind! Blow on my garden, that its fragrance
> may spread everywhere. Let my beloved come
> into his garden, and taste its choice fruits.
> —Song of Solomon 4: 16

Yep, sex is biblical! Sexual touching is an important part of a healthy marriage, which is a covenant between God and the spouses and no one else. If a spouse is denied this form of touch, he or she will have no other holy avenue to receive it. The lack of touch will also make the one denied a target for temptation.

> Do not deprive one another, except perhaps by agreement
> for a limited time, that you may devote yourselves to
> prayer; but then come together again, so that Satan may
> not tempt you because of your lack of self-control.
> —Corinthians 7:5

Physical touch is perhaps the most vital component of the EQUIP model; it will keep your personal relationships thriving with love and affection. Touch instantly connects us and bears the fruits of motivation, intimacy, security, and joy. It's so powerful that it can also be an ally for professional relationships, but it must be used with caution to avoid encroaching on others' barriers. But these positive relational builders only come to those who are present and active.

Life is too sweet and too short to express our affection with just our thumbs. Touch is meant for more than a keyboard.
—Kristin Armstrong

Growing Spiritually through Physical Touch

- James 1:22: Do not merely listen to the word, and so deceive yourselves. Do what it says.

- Acts 19:11 ESV: And God was doing extraordinary miracles by the hands of Paul.

- Mark 10:16: And he took the children in his arms, placed his hands on them and blessed them.

- Romans 16:16: Greet on another with a holy kiss. All the churches of Christ send greetings.

- Genesis 2:24: That is why a man leaves his father and mother and is united to his wife, and they become one flesh.

chapter 6
personality matrix

It's beauty that captures your attention;
personality which captures your heart.
—Oscar Wilde

I first learned about the differences in these little, heart-capturing things we're all born with called personalities back in pharmacy school. In one class, we answered questions and plotted the results on a chart to uncover our Myers-Briggs personality type. I remember talking later with other students in my class about our results. We said things like, "I think I'm an INTJ. What are you?" "Oh, I'm an ESFP." If that sounds confusing, don't worry; I doubt any of us understood what those acronyms truly meant or how to apply them. I felt the Myers-Briggs was definitely a good system but required a lot of understanding. It was difficult to get a good grasp on this personality concept after one questionnaire. However, the experience prompted me to learn more about personality assessments.

During my MBA classes, I was given the assignment of reading two books that contained personality tests. That's when I started trying to understand how to use personality temperaments to enhance my relationships and build great teams. For example, I thought I could identify a person who had a leader personality type and suggest he or she be put in charge of a group project that would make us all function better, but I had a hard time putting people into categories. And when I noticed the categories others put themselves in when filling out their personality questionnaire, I became even more confused. For example, the people who had said they were leaders would be very passive and hands-off, while those who said they were people oriented would often become frustrated with me for attempting to talk to them. I realized we could view ourselves differently from how others view us.

I was just as guilty as everyone else. My wife laughed hysterically after seeing the answers I gave on old personality questionnaires. "I can't believe you said you were laid back!" My wife knows the real me. What's interesting is that I appeared laid back at school and at work, so I picked that selection as one of my answers based on others' feedback. As my wife knows, how I appear and how I really am are sometimes complete opposites.

To compound the problem, I've found my environment, situation, and type of people I'm around can cause me to act differently; my social friends may perceive me differently from the way my work colleagues do, and they both perceive me differently from the way my family does.

What are we to do with such conflicting data? Who am I really? Am I indeed laid back? To answer such questions, I recommend starting with my Personality Matrix model, moving on to a book such as *Personality Plus*, and then even to a Myers-Briggs assessment for a deeper understanding of yourself. But whatever assessment you pick, the key to success is first getting a good, honest grasp on what you're really made of. Then embrace your findings, because it's what's inside of you that matters most.

> Positive feelings come from being honest about yourself and accepting your personality, and physical characteristics, warts and all; and, from belonging to a family that accepts you without question.
> —Willard Scott

> When Michelangelo was ready to carve the statue of David, he spent a long time in selecting the marble, for he knew the quality of the raw

material would determine the beauty of the finished product. He knew he could change the shape of the stone, but he couldn't transform the basic ingredient. Every masterpiece he made was unique, for even if he had wanted to, he would not have been able to find a duplicate piece of marble. Even if he cut a block from the same quarry, it wouldn't have been exactly the same. Similar, yes, but not the same.[77]

—Florence Littauer

The intention of the Personality Matrix is *not* to attempt to make you change your or others' personalities; I don't believe that's possible.[78] However, you can change your behavior as you borrow qualities from other personality types. But whether you try to mimic qualities you see in others or bring one of your own inner qualities to the surface, you'll still consist of your original makeup.

Our original, unique personality mixes cause us to develop our own way of dealing with relationships, but whatever those ways are, they all come with strengths and weaknesses. The Personality Matrix helps you utilize your own and others' strengths while also providing a platform to grow and improve on your weaknesses.

The topic of personality types dates back to 450 BC, when Hippocrates theorized that we are made up of different combinations of four fluids (humors) that affect our bodies in a variety of ways. In AD 190, Galen added that our behaviors have roots in the four humors, which he called temperaments. To this day, many personality tests are based on the characteristics Galen gave to these temperaments. Interestingly, most of the recent personality models are based on four categories. Even the currently popular Myers-Briggs assessment that came out in 1958 is based upon four core questions.[79]

While the Bible makes no mention of four distinct personality types, it does contain some interesting concepts. For example, God chose to have four disciples (Matthew, Mark, Luke, and John) with four unique points of view write the gospel of Jesus. Each disciple came from a different background and painted the gospel with unique brush strokes. The book of Revelation contains an account of the four horsemen who each had four faces on one head—human, eagle, lion, and ox. I know of personality test categories based on these biblical references.

Many churches and religious organizations are against personality testing, however; they feel the results are subjective, unreliable, not validated, contradicting, and misleading, and they think they take away from the Bible's teachings. I agree wholeheartedly with these objections. As mentioned earlier, I found many of the same problems when I simply tried to put people, including myself, into categories. I believe that God created us unique blends of several attributes and that we all have specific, special purposes. Even every hair on our head is accounted for.

> But even the hairs on your head are all numbered.
> —Matthew 10:30

For argument's sake, if there were indeed four categories and we all had unique blends of them, we could calculate thousands of different personality combinations. For example, you could be exactly equal in all categories and have 25 percent of each. Or you might have a mix of 50 percent of one, 20 percent of another, 18 percent of a third, and just 12 percent of the fourth. You can see where I'm going with this. No one will ever fit exactly into some kind of box we place him or her in based on some observations.

Just as Hippocrates and Galen observed thousands of years ago, people do have different personality styles and ways they deal with others, but some similarities exist that seem to repeat in those styles. Whether you believe the total number of different personality categories is two, four, eight, or more, I feel that having a tool to help make sense of the differences can be helpful. I think that other valid points of view for any situation exist, and that makes me more likely to understand and love my neighbor as the Bible teaches.

Using a four-category model makes it easy to put the characteristics into a compass-like quadrant illustration. You take two opposites, like north and south and east and west, then plot your course. But instead of north or south, personality quadrants involve thinking or doing, being passive or aggressive, and so on. Of the many different four category models I've come across and attempted to apply, I have one favorite. I like it because it was one of the first I encountered and makes it easy for me to understand my own and others' actions in relational situations.[80]

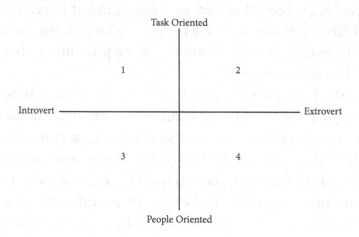

The first step is plotting the east and west coordinates by determining where you fall on the introvert to extrovert continuum.

Introvert ————————————————————— Extrovert

Most people have a good idea where they fall on this scale. However, there are some common misconceptions about what constitutes introversion and extroversion. For example, introverts are not by definition shy, antisocial, or anxious; they are energized by being alone, and their energy is drained by being around other people.[81] Introverts will lose energy as they interact with others; the more people an introvert has to deal with, the more exhausting the experience becomes, causing the introvert to appear withdrawn.

I'm an introvert; I understand how difficult social interactions can become. Throw in an event where I have the spotlight, and there's a good chance I'll have a nervous breakdown before and during the experience. I know I can't just avoid social interaction and hope to have any kind of fulfilling life, so I work on socializing as if I were working out at the gym. I know I need to do it to be healthy, but it takes a lot of motivation. Over time, I have learned to improve my social skills, and I usually appear cool, calm, and collected, though internally that's not the case.

I've avoided social interactions when I could. It's not because I'm depressed, a recluse, or unsocial; it's simply my tendency to do things that energize me versus things that drain me. I love alone time when I can recharge my batteries and process my thoughts and feelings. I enjoy analytically thinking about concepts, puzzles, problems, and strategies.

When I was a drug rep, I'd volunteer to see doctors whose offices were on the outskirts of Oklahoma because I knew I'd get two to three hours of windshield time each way, a great opportunity for introspection. While most of my extroverted sales teammates avoided windshield time at all costs, I embraced it. My stimulation is internal.

This is exactly what I see with my introverted child. He has boundless energy when at home and around people he's comfortable with, but when we take him out and he has to deal with an abundance of new people, his energy declines. He excels at problem solving, and he goes over his schoolwork to ensure he understands it correctly.

Introverted people are good for relationships because they're comfortable listening to others. They pay attention to the content so they can analyze and process it later. Introverts are good problem solvers and can usually come up with new, improved ways of doing things, therefore increasing the efficiency and productivity of the group.[82]

I also have an extroverted child who acts quiet and bored at home with the people she's very familiar with, but when she meets new people, she shows boundless energy. She will excitedly ask strangers to be her best friends. She appears outgoing, confident, and friendly, but that's not the definition of an extrovert; my introverted son is just as friendly and energetic. Extroverts are simply people energized by others and drained when alone. Their stimulation comes from the environment.[83]

My wife is an extrovert and would much rather talk with someone than spend time alone. She's not one who enjoys working a Rubik's cube. Extroverts like to talk about situations to process them. Concepts just don't seem real to my wife until she has a chance to discuss them with others[84] in detail with plenty of backstory, story, and potential future story scenarios. Extroverts are good for relationships since they can do the talking with enthusiasm. They aren't afraid of the spotlight and can sometimes help take the focus off an introvert, who is much less comfortable with it.

If you're energized by others and seek them for stimulation, you're most likely an extrovert, but if you prefer alone time to think and recharge, you're most likely an introvert. To what degree you are either depends on how strongly you identify with one temperament or the other. Some people are extreme introverts or extroverts, but others can be extroverts in certain environments and introverts in others. My wife fits this last example. She usually appears extroverted until she's around her extremely extroverted friend. Her friend's stronger temperament dominates the environment, making my wife appear less extroverted. So my wife would plot herself more toward the center of the line.

Next, we determine our north/south coordinates to see if we are task or people oriented.

One of the biggest problems with personality assessments is that we have a hard time checking boxes or filling in circles that may have perceived negative associations tied to them. We all want to think we are people oriented and make others a priority, right? How could anyone choose a task over a person? Well, task people such as I do it all the time.

At work, I have the pleasure of 200 to 300 tasks in the form of prescriptions to deal with daily as well as handling phone calls, reports, training, and interactions with employees and customers. If I spend all my resources on customer interactions and fail to get the other tasks completed, I'll have an angry boss and hundreds of upset customers to deal with.

I tend to focus too much on tasks rather than people. When I just keep checking prescriptions, I miss out on opportunities to make a positive impact on my customer relationships. I could benefit by borrowing some people-oriented behavior on occasion. I have to keep a constant check on myself or I'll fill my entire day with tasks.

But remember that there's no wrong or right when it comes to personality assessments or this Personality Matrix; there's just an honest assessment of behavioral tendencies that leads to opportunities to grow and discover options. Every personality has strengths and weakness. Knowing what yours are allows you to take advantage of the strengths and overcome the weaknesses. The key is balance.

Task-oriented people will almost always have either a mental or physical to-do list running their days.[85] I post a task list for the day on my computer screen. In the morning, I check my e-mails and jot down in bullet points what I need to accomplish. The notes are always tasks such as "Fax report to district office" and never things such as "Talk to your employees about their feelings." I start knocking my tasks off one by one and crossing them off the list. The act of drawing a line through a bullet point is like a two-second massage.

As I work and go through life, I constantly think about how I can increase my productivity and efficiency so I'll complete more tasks in less time. The more efficient I get, the more likely it is I'll achieve my long list of detailed life goals. If you're a task-oriented person, you're probably thinking, *Yep, that's how you do it!* But if you're person oriented, you're probably thinking, *This sounds like a complete waste of time.*

Task people spend energy coming up with goals and a detailed roadmap to achieve them. They spend time and energy thinking of ways to improve their productivity and efficiency.[86] They also spend even more energy making daily checklists to ensure they're on track and making progress toward their goals.

Task people are good for relationships since they accomplish many things for the group; they get things done correctly. But when task people neglect the other group members as they tenaciously check off their lists, they risk ending up with no group members to accomplish things for.

My wife is person oriented. I can count on one hand how many lists I've seen her make. And those she did make never left the house with her, including her one grocery list! It's insane to me that someone can shop for groceries without a list. I almost had a heart attack just thinking about it as I typed that sentence.

People-oriented personalities tend to focus on the needs of the people around them.[87] My wife likes to build relationships and keep everyone happy. She values fairness and feelings as meaningful life goals. She often asks me if the current task I'm working on will even matter in ten years.

Shortly after we were married, I thought I'd have my wife organize a reception party for our close friends and family. I didn't have a good understanding of the whole task/people concept. I thought that since I would love to plan such a party, she would too. However, the task was so draining on her and her body that she came down with strep throat. By the time the reception started, she was thin, pale, feverish, and about to faint. I had given her a people-oriented person's worst nightmare—a month of planning and organizing tasks. It would have been the equivalent of her having me, the introvert/tasker, spend a month randomly visiting all the guests to get a good handle on their thoughts and feelings about our marriage. I would have fainted. Having learned from this experience, I'm the one who plans and organizes our events.

Person-oriented people talk about others' feelings and emotions and remember them.[88] Every time I ask my favorite person-oriented employee, Sarah, anything about what someone had told her, she can usually tell me only the emotional details. She wouldn't be able to tell me what position her son played on his football team, but she could give me the full story on how he felt about playing.

People-oriented personalities are good for relationships since they uncover the feelings and emotions of the situation. They keep things fair and ensure everyone remains happy. They spend their time and energy meeting the needs of those around them and making them feel important.

If tasks and lists run your day, put yourself at the top of the line. If your relations and feelings run your day, put yourself at the bottom. How far you put yourself away from the center depends on how strongly you identify with tasks or with people. Now connect the two dots. Whatever quadrant your new line lies in is most likely your dominant temperament or personality type.

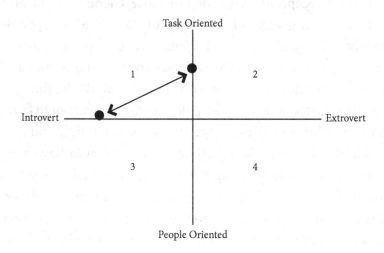

This is what my line looks like, so I land in quadrant 1, with my natural introverted task orientation. That's my comfort zone. When I can function in this quadrant, I'm happy and productive and can understand and deal with relationships with this perspective. Working in others areas of the matrix,

(2, 3, and 4) can be difficult and stressful for me, as is dealing with those whose natural orientation puts them in one of those other quadrants (potentially 75 percent of the people out there). An extrovert and people-oriented person will have a completely opposite way of dealing with the same situation than I do.

This scenario is the exact dynamic of my marriage; my wife is extroverted and people-oriented. Opposites attract, but in some situations, she and I may think the other is being difficult and wanting to accomplish a different objective.

Dealing with People you Can't Stand by Rick Brinkman and Rick Kirschner explains how we can become difficult when something or someone hinders our goals. Their book will help you understand why others may be less than positive about any given situation and will help you not turn into someone whom people can't stand. It has been great for our marriage and helps my wife put up with me.

Overlapping Brinkman's and Kirschner's intention groups[89] onto the model looks like this. So people in quadrant 1, like myself, usually strive to get their tasks not just done but done "just right". And we can become less than positive when that's not the case.

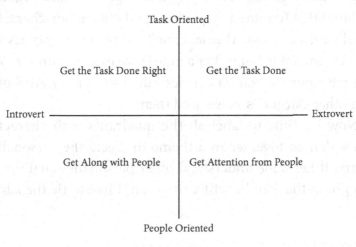

Task Oriented

Get the Task Done Right | Get the Task Done

Introvert — Extrovert

Get Along with People | Get Attention from People

People Oriented

When my wife and I were dating, she'd often come to my place to hang out on a Saturday. I would excitedly tell her about all the tasks I had planned for the day. She would look at me with a "Are you kidding me, Dude?" expression. Some of the tasks I had planned included my doing homework while she watched TV; that of course was the opposite of the reason she came over—for us to get to know each other.

She often tried to complete tasks for me so we could move on to something more meaningful for her. But not getting my tasks done in the way or the order I had envisioned went against my intentions of getting things done right. (And as any Group 1 member will attest to, my way is the right way.) We'd end up frustrated with each other.

One time when I left her in the living room while I completed some tasks, she picked up *Dealing with People You Can't Stand*, which I had been reading. It explained everything to her! She was relieved I wasn't trying to avoid her but was just task driven. She asked me to discuss the book. We soon realized our problem and agreed on a compromise to meet each other's needs.

Instead of giving you a long list of positive and negative attributes that fit into each quadrant, I'll offer a four-character model with a common theme. I don't feel personality types are a box we end up in but rather a matrix we move around in. We start with our natural tendencies but then borrow attributes from other categories as we need them.

Now it's time to label all the quadrants with character names that go together in a theme to create the Personality Matrix. It helps me understand other personality qualities of each group that can benefit a situation. I like to tie the labels up in a common theme since I feel we all have a mix of these styles already in us to utilize and help create balance.

Some are easier and more natural to express than others; if you placed a dot on the end of a line, you would probably find it difficult to get to the other side of the matrix. But when I make the effort to get all four characters invested in a relationship, the results have usually helped me achieve balance and resonance.

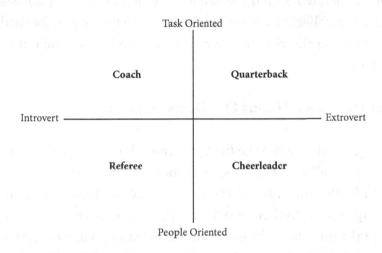

This Personality Matrix contains the people who make up a successful football team. However, these descriptions are just an example of how to think about this particular team and not absolute definitions. For example, a referee can be an extrovert in the real world but for the purposes of this matrix will be a person-oriented introvert. In this matrix, they each contribute their best to score touchdowns in the coveted Relationship Resonance Bowl.[90]

Coaches: Analytical, Serious Planners

Coaches are on the sidelines but manage the game with a serious demeanor. They are constantly assessing the present situation after weeks of analyzing film and planning. They look down at their list of plays and send one in to be executed exactly as it was drawn up. Any deviation from the play design will not be tolerated even if the result is a touchdown. They appear calm and collected while the million scenarios of possible bad outcomes to the play nearly cause them to call a time out to reassess.

Quarterbacks: Hands On, Decisive Leaders

Quarterbacks are the field generals who motivate the team with pep talks in the huddle as they call out the play. They confidently walk toward the defense and set their players in the right positions before yelling "Hike!" They receive the snap and take the fate of the game into their hands. They run, pass, or hand the ball to get it into the end zone. Their goal is a touchdown in any way, shape, or form, so deviations from the play design will be justified.

Referees: Quiet, Watchful Peacekeepers

Referees are the peacekeepers; they enforce the rules and keep tempers from flaring. They keep a watchful eye on the players and coaches to ensure everyone's getting along in the name of good sportsmanship. The only time they talk is when someone breaks a rule and they calmly explain the infraction. Otherwise, they simply use body language and their whistles to keep the game flowing. They keep their composure in the midst of thousands of screaming fans, players, and coaches. Their goal is to ensure everyone is getting along while having a quality time.

Cheerleaders: Enthusiastic, Flashy Encouragers

Cheerleaders are the emotional catalyst of the game. They draw the spectators' attention with their uniforms, accessories, and body movements. They initiate emotional and heartfelt cheers to motivate and inspire their teams. With boundless energy and loud voices, they continue to support their teams no matter what the score is. Their goal is to bring out the positive emotions in everyone present.

The way I think about personality difference is through this Personality Matrix. Each character has equal importance and impact on the outcome —relationships. When all four work together, the results are phenomenal. I try to constantly remind myself to balance my relations with all four groups. I am a natural coach and therefore attempt to incorporate more quarterback, referee, and cheerleading into my interactions.

I do this in two ways. First, I try to surround myself with people whose natural temperament is something other than a coach. This way, I can focus on my strengths and let others focus on theirs. For example, I married a cheerleader, so I can lead in planning and organizing while she can lead in socializing and bringing our positive emotions out.

At first, I would always struggle with people with anything but a coach personality. I would think there must have been something wrong with them. Why would these people not get excited about staying home to plan and organize? But when I was with a group of coaches, I spent a lot of time butting heads because all coaches want things to go their way. But after learning about personality differences, I have appreciated the other styles. It opens my heart and eyes to alternative points of view.

Whomever I have surrounded myself with, I've always tried to learn from their expertise. Even when I'm in the presence of other coaches, I can learn a great deal about how to plan and organize even better.

Second, I attempt to mimic the other types. I've painfully realized I can't change my internal makeup and become someone I'm not, but I can enhance some of my inner cheerleader. For example, I can work on incorporating some cheerleader behavior and enthusiastically encourage others to keep talking to me.

Nothing's wrong with a bunch of coaches working or living together; I just found it beneficial to sprinkle in some occasional alternative characters. Even as difficult and unnatural as it is for me, I still make the effort in order to enhance my relationships. At work, I have a cheerleader standing one foot to my right who excitedly greets customers as she takes their prescriptions. The coach and cheerleader are perfectly balanced, giving their customers excellent service. But when my cheerleader is on vacation, I usually have another coach as her replacement. To keep the customer relations positive, I incorporate a lot more cheerleading into my day.

If a sports theme is not your cup of tea, I offer an alternative Personality Matrix theme: editors, directors, writers, and actors. As before, these descriptions are not absolute definitions but rather a way to think about and apply this matrix. Together, this team creates a beautiful, award-winning movie called Relationship Resonance.

Editors: Detailed, Organized Perfectionists

Editors take all the film and covert it into the final production. They cut out piece after piece to get to the bottom line or main point of the scene. Editors meticulously work out the time and sound constraints to fit everything together perfectly. They may spend hours alone working on a two-second audio clip to get it just right.

Directors: Strong Willed, Blunt Commanders

Directors control the stage as they motivate the actors to bring the story to life. They position the actors and set things in motion with a loud "Action!" Once directors feel a scene is finished, they will abruptly yell, "Cut!" and move on. They may modify the script in order to complete the scene in a timely fashion. Any substandard performance by the actors will be handled swiftly and bluntly.

Writers: Patient, Empathetic Observers

Writers reflect on their observations and insights to create emotional stories they know the world will enjoy. Often in seclusion, they patiently and persistently type on their keyboard to create their masterpiece with little regard to deadlines. They know how to use words to make it easy for everyone else to understand the feelings of the stories they create.

Actors: Emotional, Charismatic Storytellers

Actors become the stories as they say their lines. They take the feelings and emotions from the script and bring them to life with their skill. They are masters of facial expressions, vocal tone, and body movement. They will powerfully captivate the attention of an audience as they transfer the emotions to the viewers. Winning an award for their performance is a dream come true.

I tend to bring the editing/coach into my relationships. I analyze interactions and situations and look for clues to a deeper understanding rather than directly asking others about their feelings. I have good planning and organizing skills that make my and others' lives more efficient but often fail to make our lives more emotional. I'm learning to enthusiastically cheer, be more direct and decisive in my actions, socialize, and accept that it's sometimes better to get along than to just get things done.

No one is ever wrong or right when it comes to the personality styles they choose to go with for any situation. The Bible makes reference for us to each decide when the time is right for an alternative point of view in Ecclesiastes 3.

There is a time for everything, and a season
for every activity under the heavens:
a time to be born and a time to die, a time
to plant and a time to uproot,
a time to kill and a time to heal,
a time to tear down and a time to build,
a time to weep and a time to laugh, a time
to mourn and a time to dance,
a time to scatter stones and a time to gather them,
a time to embrace and a time to refrain from embracing,
a time to search and a time to give up,
a time to keep and a time to throw away,
a time to tear and a time to mend,
a time to be silent and a time to speak,
a time to love and a time to hate,
a time for war and a time for peace.

Growing Spiritually through the Personality Matrix

- Psalm 119:15: I will meditate on your precepts and fix my eyes on your ways.

- Psalm 144:1 Of David, Blessed be the Lord, my rock, who trains my hands for war, and my fingers for battle.

- Proverbs 15:1: A soft answer turns away wrath, but a harsh word stirs up anger.

- Hebrews 10:24: Let us consider how to stir up one another to love and good works.

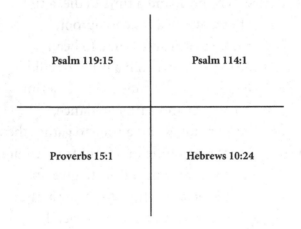

Psalm 119:15	Psalm 114:1
Proverbs 15:1	Hebrews 10:24

conclusion
putting it all together

Using the Relationship Resonance system has allowed me to make a positive impact on my personal, professional, and spiritual connections. Using the EQUIP model and Personality Matrix has helped me to understand and improve on my weaknesses while providing the platform for me to serve others. I constantly do mental run downs of the variables to ensure they all get applied to my relationships as frequently as possible.

For example, in my personal relationships, I often realize I haven't been getting much physical touch into my interactions, so I make an effort to act on all my thoughts of love by stepping up the hugs and kisses I give my family. I look at where I'm investing my resources and make decisions based on which ones have more EQUIP value.

So now, I golf much less and ballroom dance with my wife instead as I move into the quarterback and actor matrixes. Dancing provides me an opportunity to literally take the lead to encourage her grace and beauty, spend quality time together, show my understanding of her need to do something she loves, invest my time and treasure into our relationship, and physically and passionately touch her Argentine tango style.

I have also learned to ease back on my coaching tendencies and embrace the quarterback, cheerleader, and referee roles. When one of my children spills the milk, I remember to hug him or her and say all will be okay rather than breaking down exactly how and why things went wrong. When my wife sees I'm going out of my natural element to improve my relationships with our children, it resonates with her.

In my professional relationships, I do the same thing. I realize I need to encourage my employees for working tirelessly hard for me, so I thank them for everything they do as I explain what a positive impact they have on our company, me, and my family. Then I invest in little tokens of appreciation like drinks or pizza. I've learned to let cheerleaders be cheerleaders and not expect them to be quarterbacks. But at the same time, I push myself, the coach, to temporarily fill in as quarterback as necessary.

Spiritually, I have realized that God wants us to EQUIP him as well, so I praise him with hands held high during worship services and thank him for all my blessings. I spend quality time meditating in prayer. I show understanding to my neighbor in his name. I invested my talents helping others in his name. I actively seek him and his word.

When I'm forced to deal with a difficult or upset person, the system not only provides a means to handle the situation but also usually reverses the polarity. I've learned to lookout for an upset customer like a coach surveying the opposing team. I analyze my customers' tone, body language, and verbal content. When I identify and encounter upset customers, I can confidently engage them like a quarterback walking up to the line of scrimmage instead of ignoring them or passing the buck. I attempt to offer them a moment of quality time as I behave like a referee and calmly listen to them voice their complaints without taking it personally. And then I move into a cheerleader role; I encourage the dialog with positive language and thank them for telling me about the issue and show them sincere understanding.

I explain how I'll prevent reoccurrences of any problem and end by offering a handshake.

Thank you for investing your time and resources on this book! I pray the information I gave will help to make all your relationships positively resonate.

quick reference

Encourage: Praise and Compliments / Appreciation / Positive
Language

Quality Time: Full / Focused / Uninterrupted

Understanding: Avoid Barriers / Open Your Heart / Listen /
Think/ Show Understanding

Invest: Detox and Invest in Health / Invest Time, Tongue,
Treasure, Talent, Tenacity / Protect Investments with Truth
and Humility

Physical Touch: Be Present and Active / Respect Boundaries /
Physically Touch

Personality Matrix: Coach / Quarterback / Referee /
Cheerleader—Editor / Director/ Performer / Writer

about the author

Doug Hacking received a doctorate of pharmacy from the University of Oklahoma in 2000 and a master's of business administration from the University of Central Oklahoma in 2005. He is a former pharmaceutical sales representative and works as a pharmacist, adjunct faculty, and relational consultant. He has over fifteen years of professional teaching experience and has devoted over twenty years to researching, practicing, and creating his Relationship Resonance system.

Dr. Hacking is a recent recipient of the University of Oklahoma's Outstanding Preceptor and the CVS Health Paragon awards. Doug resides with his wife and three children in Edmond, Oklahoma, where he attends and serves LifeChurch.

endnotes

1   "Peter McWilliams Quote." *BrainyQuote*. Xplore, n.d. Web. 11 June 2015.

2   Hatmaker, Jen. *Interrupted: When Jesus Wrecks Your Comfortable Chrisitianity*. N.p.: n.p., n.d. Print.

3   The ideas for this section came from ESPN films *30 for 30: Survive* and *Advance*, directed by Jonathan Hock.

4   *Growing Spiritually: Interview with Kevin Durant and Carl Lentz*. By Craig Groeschel. Lifechurch.TV. 02 December 2013.

5   *Comedy Performance*. By Adam Yenser. The Ice House, Pasadena. 07 Nov. 2010. Performance.

6   Morgan, Rebecca L. *Calming Upset Customers*. Las Altos, CA: Crisp Publications, 1989. Print.

7   *Oklahoma Football Legends Reunion*. Perf. Barry Switzer and Spencer Tillman. Nashville, Tenn. Gabriel Sports Reunion, 2003. DVD.

8   Goleman, Daniel, Richard E. Boyatzis, and Annie McKee. *Primal Leadership: Realizing the Power of Emotional Intelligence*. Boston, MA: Harvard Business School, 2002. Print.

9   Goleman, Daniel, Richard E. Boyatzis, and Annie McKee. *Primal Leadership: Realizing the Power of Emotional Intelligence*. Boston, MA: Harvard Business School, 2002. Print.

10 Hargrave, Jan Latiolais. *Let Me See Your Body Talk*. Dubuque, IA: Kendall/Hunt Pub., 1996. Print.

11 Okstaff. "Breakfasting with Reba McEntire." *OK Magazine*. N.p., 09 Oct. 2007. Web. 11 June 2015.

12 Cloud, Susan. "How to Be Liberated." *The Capital* [Maryland] 1973: n. pag. Print.

13 Macmillan, A. "12 Reasons to Stop Multitasking Now." *Fox News*. FOX News Network, 18 June 2013. Web. 11 June 2015.

14 "Frequent Multitaskers Are Bad at It." *Frequent Multitaskers Are Bad at It*. U News Center Staff, 23 Jan. 2013. Web. 16 June 2015.

15 Leitko, Aaron. "The Dangers of Multi-tasking." *Washington Post*. The Washington Post, 01 Aug. 2011. Web. 16 June 2015.

16 Brown, Oger. "Multitasking Gets You There Later." *InfoQ*. N.p., 29 June 2010. Web. 16 June 2015.
17 Nguyen, Steve. "Multitasking Doesn't Work." *Workplace Psychology*. N.p., 04 Apr. 2011. Web. 16 June 2015.
18 Macmillan, A. "12 Reasons to Stop Multitasking Now." *Fox News*. FOX News Network, 18 June 2013. Web. 11 June 2015.
19 Weinschenk, Susan. "The True Cost Of Multi-Tasking." *Psychology Today*. Brain Wise, 18 Sept. 2012. Web. 16 June 2015.
20 Santosus, Megan. "Multitasking Wastes Time and Money." *CIO*. N.p., 15 Sept. 2003. Web. 16 June 2015.
21 Macmillan, A. "12 Reasons to Stop Multitasking Now." *Fox News*. FOX News Network, 18 June 2013. Web. 11 June 2015.
22 Macmillan, A. "12 Reasons to Stop Multitasking Now." *Fox News*. FOX News Network, 18 June 2013. Web. 11 June 2015.
23 Cherry, Kendra. "The Cognitive Costs of Multitasking." About.com, 2015. Web. 16 June 2015.
24 Brown, Roger. "Multitasking Gets You There Later." *InfoQ*. N.p., 29 June 2010. Web. 16 June 2015.
25 Macmillan, A. "12 Reasons to Stop Multitasking Now." *Fox News*. FOX News Network, 18 June 2013. Web. 11 June 2015.
26 Merrill, Douglas. "Why Multitasking Doesn't Work." *Forbes*. Forbes Magazine, 17 Aug. 2012. Web. 16 June 2015.
27 Merrill, Douglas. "Why Multitasking Doesn't Work." *Forbes*. Forbes Magazine, 17 Aug. 2012. Web. 16 June 2015.
28 Macmillan, A. "12 Reasons to Stop Multitasking Now." *Fox News*. FOX News Network, 18 June 2013. Web. 11 June 2015.
29 Cherry, Kendra. "The Cognitive Costs of Multitasking." About.com, 2015. Web. 16 June 2015.
30 Macmillan, A. "12 Reasons to Stop Multitasking Now." *Fox News*. FOX News Network, 18 June 2013. Web. 11 June 2015.
31 Goleman, Daniel, Richard E. Boyatzis, and Annie McKee. *Primal Leadership: Realizing the Power of Emotional Intelligence*. Boston, MA: Harvard Business School, 2002. Print.
32 Freiberg, Kevin, and Jackie Freiberg. *Nuts!: Southwest Airlines' Crazy Recipe for Business and Personal Success*. Austin, TX: Bard, 1996. Print.
33 Hatmaker, Jen. *Interrupted: When Jesus Wrecks Your Comfortable Chrisitianity*. N.p.: n.p., n.d. Print. Pg. XII
34 Covey, Stephen R. *The Seven Habits of Highly Effective People: Restoring the Character Ethic*. New York: Simon and Schuster, 1989. Print.

35 Nadig, Larry Alan. "Effective Listening." *Effective Listening*. N.p., 19 July 2010. Web. 16 June 2015.

36 *Dictionary.com*. Dictionary.com, n.d. Web. 16 June 2015.

37 "Active Listening." *U.S. Department of State*. U.S. Department of State, n.d. Web. 16 June 2015.

38 Winter, Katy. "'Why Can't the Phrase "run like a Girl" Still Mean Win the Race?': Moving Video Shows How Young Women Are Affected by Gender Stereotyping." *Mail Online*. Associated Newspapers, 30 June 2014. Web. 16 June 2015.

39 Lee, Dick, and Delmar Hatesohl. "Listening: Our Most Used Communication Skill." *CM150 Listening: Our Most Used Communications Skill*. N.p., 30 Oct. 1993. Web. 17 June 2015.

40 Lee, Dick, and Delmar Hatesohl. "Listening: Our Most Used Communication Skill." *CM150 Listening: Our Most Used Communications Skill*. N.p., 30 Oct. 1993. Web. 17 June 2015.

41 Lee, Dick, and Delmar Hatesohl. "Listening: Our Most Used Communication Skill." *CM150 Listening: Our Most Used Communications Skill*. N.p., 30 Oct. 1993. Web. 17 June 2015.

42 "Apostolic Christian Counseling and Family Services: Search Results." *Apostolic Christian Counseling and Family Services: Search Results*. N.p., 2008. Web. 17 June 2015.

43 "Apostolic Christian Counseling and Family Services: Search Results." *Apostolic Christian Counseling and Family Services: Search Results*. N.p., 2008. Web. 17 June 2015.

44 Hargrave, Jan Latiolais. *Let Me See Your Body Talk*. Dubuque, IA: Kendall/Hunt Pub., 1996. Print.

45 Webb, David, and Craig-James Baxter. "Guide To Detecting Deceit and Evaluating Honesty." *Guide To Detecting Deceit and Evaluating Honesty*. N.p., 2012. Web. 17 June 2015.

46 Burton, Roy. "THE ART OF ACTIVE LISTENING." *THE ART OF ACTIVE LISTENING*. Selfgrowth.com, n.d. Web. 17 June 2015.

47 Masin, Pam. "4 Amazing Health Benefits Of Helping Others." *The Huffington Post*. TheHuffingtonPost.com, 28 Dec. 2013. Web. 17 June 2015.

48 Groeschel, Craig. *Soul Detox: Clean Living in a Contaminated World*. Grand Rapids, MI: Zondervan, 2012. Print.

49 Warner, Jennifer. "Exercise Fights Fatigue, Boosts Energy." *WebMD*. WebMD, 03 Nov. 2006. Web. 18 June 2015.

50   Healthwise. "Healthy Eating-Topic Overview." *WebMD*. WebMD, 14 Nov. 2014. Web. 18 June 2015.

51   Healthline Staff. "5 Benefits of Healthy Habits." *Healthline*. N.p., 01 Apr. 2013. Web. 18 June 2015.

52   Brook, Mary. "Training Blog All about Training, Training Industry & Learning." *Training Blog*. N.p., 03 Oct. 2012. Web. 18 June 2015.

53   "Journal of Managerial Psychology." *Fitness and Leadership: Is There a Relationship?: Fitness and Leadership: Is There a Relationship?: : Vol 17, No 4*. N.p., n.d. Web. 18 June 2015.

54   "Addictions and Recovery : Test Yourself." *Addictions and Recovery*. N.p., n.d. Web. 18 June 2015. <http://www.addictionsandrecovery.org/addiction-self-test.htm>.

55   Duhigg, Charles. *The Power of Habit: Why We Do What We Do in Life and Business*. New York: Random House, 2012. Print.

56   Morgan, Rebecca L. *Calming Upset Customers*. Las Altos, CA: Crisp Publications, 1989. Print.

57   Harvey, Steve, and Jeffrey Johnson. *Act like a Success, Think like a Success: Discovering Your Gift and the Way to Life's Riches*. N.p.: n.p., n.d. Print.

58   Harvey, Steve, and Jeffrey Johnson. *Act like a Success, Think like a Success: Discovering Your Gift and the Way to Life's Riches*. N.p.: n.p., n.d. Print. Pg. 9.

59   Engel, Beverly. "The Power of Apology." *Psychology Today*. N.p., 01 July 2002. Web. 18 June 2015.

60   Durant, Kevin. "Kevin Durant: The Oklahoma City Thunder Star's Complete MVP Speech." *NewsOK.com*. N.p., 13 May 2014. Web. 18 June 2015.

61   O. Zur and N. Nordmarken, "To Touch or Not to Touch: Exploring the Myth of Prohibition on Touch," in *Psychotherapy and Counseling*, www.zurinstitute.com/touchintherapy.html retrieved January 1, 2015.

62   Goleman, Daniel. "The Experience of Touch: Research Points to a Critical Role." *The New York Times*. The New York Times, 01 Feb. 1988. Web. 18 June 2015.

63   O. Zur and N. Nordmarken, "To Touch or Not to Touch: Exploring the Myth of Prohibition on Touch," in *Psychotherapy and Counseling*, www.zurinstitute.com/touchintherapy.html retrieved January 1, 2015.

64   Ofri, Danielle. "Not on the Doctor's Checklist, but Touch Matters." *The New York Times*. The New York Times, 02 Aug. 2010. Web. 18 June 2015.

65   Carey, Benedict. "Evidence That Little Touches Do Mean So Much." *The New York Times*. The New York Times, 22 Feb. 2010. Web. 18 June 2015.

66   O. Zur and N. Nordmarken, "To Touch or Not to Touch: Exploring the Myth of Prohibition on Touch," in *Psychotherapy and Counseling*, www.zurinstitute.com/touchintherapy.html retrieved January 1, 2015.

67   O. Zur and N. Nordmarken, "To Touch or Not to Touch: Exploring the Myth of Prohibition on Touch," in *Psychotherapy and Counseling*, www.zurinstitute.com/touchintherapy.html retrieved January 1, 2015.

68   "Be Curious, Not Invasive . . .Physical Contact & Personal Boundaries." *Be Curious, Not Invasive . . .Physical Contact & Personal Boundaries*. Dartmouth College, 22 Oct. 2008. Web. 18 June 2015.

69   Cloud, Henry. "The Simple Scoop on Boundaries." *Cloud Townsend Resources*. N.p., 03 July 2000. Web. 18 June 2015.

70   Smallwood, Linda. "Boundaries and Physical Touch in Counselling." *Suite*. N.p., 15 June 2011. Web. 18 June 2015.

71   Dunn, B. "Physical Contact at Work: What Are The Boundaries?" *Careerbuilder*. N.p., 20 Jan. 2010. Web. 18 June 2015.

72   Moll, Rob. "The Importance of Human Touch." *Rob Moll Author*. N.p., 09 Mar. 2010. Web. 30 June 2015.

73   Lee, Robert, and Matt Ha. "Physical Touch Is Important in a Relationship - Vancity Buzz." *Vancity Buzz*. N.p., 12 Feb. 2011. Web. 18 June 2015.

74   Chapman, Gary D. *The Five Love Languages: How to Express Heartfelt Commitment to Your Mate*. Chicago: Northfield Pub., 1995. Print.

75   Gulledge, Andrew K., Robert F. Stahmann, and Colwick M. Wilson. "Seven Types Of Nonsexual Romantic Physical Affection Among Brigham Young University Students 1." *Psychological Reports* 95.2 (2004): 609-14. Web. 18 June 2015

76   Whitbourne, Susan Krauss. "Seven Types of Physical Affection in Relationships." *Psychology Today*. N.p., 28 Jan. 2014. Web. 18 June 2015.

77   Littauer, Florence. *Personality plus*. Tarrytown, NY: F.H. Revell, 1992. Print.

78   Warfield, Hal. "FAQs about Temperament and Personality Types." *FAQs about Temperament and Personality Types*. Selfgrowth.com, n.d. Web. 18 June 2015.

79   Ateel, Saqib Ali. "History of Personality Tests Up to Kiersy Temperament Sorter." *Personality and Aptitude Career Tests*. N.p., n.d. Web. 18 June 2015.

80 Littauer, Florence. *Personality plus*. Tarrytown, NY: F.H. Revell, 1992. Print.

81 Bainbridge, Carol. "Introvert Definition and Characteristics." About. com, n.d. Web. 18 June 2015.

82 Ehman, Mandi. "Understanding Your Personality: Balancing Tasks and People." *The Art of Simple*. N.p., 07 Sept. 2011. Web. 18 June 2015.

83 Bainbridge, Carol. "What Is an Extrovert? - Definition of Term." About.com, n.d. Web. 18 June 2015.

84 Bainbridge, Carol. "What Is an Extrovert? - Definition of Term." About.com, n.d. Web. 18 June 2015.

85 Ehman, Mandi. "Understanding Your Personality: Balancing Tasks and People." *The Art of Simple*. N.p., 07 Sept. 2011. Web. 18 June 2015.

86 Ehman, Mandi. "Understanding Your Personality: Balancing Tasks and People." *The Art of Simple*. N.p., 07 Sept. 2011. Web. 18 June 2015.

87 Ehman, Mandi. "Understanding Your Personality: Balancing Tasks and People." *The Art of Simple*. N.p., 07 Sept. 2011. Web. 18 June 2015.

88 Ehman, Mandi. "Understanding Your Personality: Balancing Tasks and People." *The Art of Simple*. N.p., 07 Sept. 2011. Web. 18 June 2015.

89 Brinkman, Rick, and Rick Kirschner. *Dealing with People You Can't Stand: How to Bring out the Best in People at Their Worst*. New York: McGraw-Hill, 1994. Print.

90 The descriptions used for the Personality Matrix themes were founded on Galen's categorical personality traits found on www. prepareforpsychologicaltest.com under "The Choleric, Melancholy, Phlegmatic, and Sanguine Personality Types." Web. 18 June 2015.